# Fit to Play™ Golf

## Improve Fitness & Lower Your Score

by Nina Nittinger & Carl Petersen

4/9/19

Adam:

Here's to many more rounds together - both at Capilano and abroad!

Regards, Russell

NEUER SPORTVERLAG

# Table of Contents

## CHAPTER 1
## MAKING YOURSELF A BETTER GOLFER

Introduction, Making Yourself a Better Golfer    8
The S's of Smart Training    12
- S1—Structured Training (On and Off the Golf Course)    13
- S2—Structured Physical and Medical Assessments    15
- S3—Structured Environment    17
- S4—Structured Mental Training    18
- S5—Structured Yearly Planning and Periodization    19
- S6—Structured Injury Prevention and Recovery    20

## CHAPTER 2
## THE ABCS OF SMART TRAINING FOR GOLFERS

The ABCs of Smart Training for Golfers    24
- A1—Athletic stance and alignment    24
- A2—Adaptive training    26
- B1—Balance exercises    27
- B2—Balanced training programs    29
- C1—Consistent training    29
- C2—Connect your core    30
- C3—Chain exercises: closed,
  partially closed, and open    32
- D1—Diversity in drills and training    34
- D2—Dynamic hip extension exercises    35
- E1—Exercise at a slow and
  controlled tempo (sometimes)    35
- E2—Excellent form    36
- F1—Functional training    36
- F2—Flexible and fun planning    37

## CHAPTER 3
## DYNAMIC WARM-UP & COOL-DOWN GUIDELINES

Dynamic Warm-Up & Cool-Down Guidelines    40
Sample Dynamic Warm-Up    42
- W1—General (aerobic) & Knee Warm Up    42
- W2—Balance & Leg Warm-Up    43
- W3—Lower Core & Leg Warm-Up    43
- W4—Upper Core & Shoulder Warm-Up    44
- W5—CNS (central nervous system)    45
- W6—Muscle Tendon Warm-Up    46
Quick Sample Warm-Ups    47
Cool-Down & Post-Training Conform Stretching    48

## CHAPTER 4
## ON COURSE GOLF SPECIFIC WARM-UP

On Course Golf Specific Warm-Up    52
- General Warm-Up    52
- Be Prepared    52
- Warm-Up Program    54
- The Driving Range    58
- 8-12 Minute Warm-up    60

## CHAPTER 5
## STRONG & STABLE PLATFORM = BETTER SWING

Strong & Stable Platform = Better Swing    64
- Importance of Transversus Abdominus    66
Switching on Your Core    66
Precautions    67
Basework & Bridging A    68
- Base Work Supine / Lying on your back
  Tighten & Leg Slide    68
- Base Work Supine / Lying on your back
  Tighten & Leg Fall Out    69
- Base Work Supine / Lying on your back
  Tighten & Scapular Retractions    69
- Clamshell Hip Abduction    70
- Side Lying Hip Adduction    70
- Supine Bridging / Lying on your back    71
- Quadruped Bridge / Kneeling on all fours    71
- Quadruped Bridge & Single Arm raises    72
- Quadruped Bridge & Single Leg raises    72
- Prone Bridging & Hip Twist    73
- Lateral Bridging    73
Basework & Bridging B    74
- Base Work Supine / Lying on your back
  Tighten & Leg March    74
- Base Work Supine / Lying on your back
  Tighten & Arm/Leg March    75
- Side Lying Hip Abduction    75
- Supine Bridging & Ball Squeeze    76
- Supine Bridging & Shoulder/Scapular Retractions    76
- Quadruped Bridge with Rocking Movements    77
- Quadruped Bridge & Torso Rotation    77
- Prone Bridging on Forearms & Knees    78
- Prone Bridging & Single Arm Raise    78
- Prone Bridging & Single Leg Raise    79
- Lateral Bridging with Hip Raise    79

**Basework & Bridging C** 80
- Base Work Supine / Lying on your back
  Tighten & Scapular Retractions 80
- Supine Bridging & Double Arm Diagonal Pull 81
- Quadruped Bridge & Knee Circles 81
- Quadruped Bridge Opposite Arm & Leg raises 82
- Quadruped Bridge & Torso Rotations
  with Band Resistance 82
- Prone Bridging on Forearms & Toes 83
- Prone Bridging with Single Arm & Leg Raise 83
- Prone Bridging with Torso Rotation & Arm Raise 84
- Lateral Bridging with Knee Drive & Arm Raise 84
- Lateral Bridging with Arm & Leg Raise 85
**Ball, Bands & Balance Bridging A** 86
- Quadruped Bridging with Wobble Board 86
- Prone Bridging on Knees or
  Toes Forearms on BOSU® ball 87
- Prone Bridging & Knees Up
  Forearms on BOSU® ball 87
- Supine Bridging & Ball Squeeze
  Feet on Unstable Base 88
- Lateral Bridging on Unstable Base 88
- Lateral Bridging on Unstable Base with Leg Raise 89
- Supine Bridge & Shoulder Retractions 3 Positions 89
- Supine Bridge with Ball Squeeze & Diagonal Pulls 90
- Sit Downs / Eccentric Abdominals 90
**Ball, Bands & Balance Bridging B** 92
- Quadruped Bridging & Push-Ups
  on Unstable Base 92
- Supine Bridging Feet on Unstable Base 93
- Lateral Bridging on Unstable Base with Knee Drive 93
- Kneeling Resisted Hip Internal Rotation 94
- Kneeling Resisted Hip External Rotation 94
- Seated Horizontal Torso Twists 95
- Lateral Bridging with Resisted Arm Raise 95
- Supine Bridge & Upper Torso Twist Holding a Ball 96
- Supine Bridge & Hamstring Pull Ball between Knees 96
- Prone Bridge Feet on Ball & Knee Tuck 97
- Lateral Bridging on Physio Ball & Leg Lift 97
**Ball, Bands & Balance Bridging C** 98
- Quadruped Bridging & Push-Ups
  on Unstable Base 98
- Supine Bridging with Balls, Bands & Torso Rotation 99
- Lateral Bridging on Unstable Base with
  Arm & Leg Raise 99
- Seated Hip Internal Rotation & Adduction 100
- Seated Hip External Rotation & Adduction 100
- Seated Diagonal Torso Twists 101
- Supine Bridge with Ball Squeeze & Diagonal Pulls 101
- Supine Bridge & Torso Rotation with Ball Squeeze 102

- Supine Bridge over Physio Ball & Diagonal Pulls 102
- Supine Bridge with Back Extension &
  Arm Extension 103
**Upper Core Stability-Proper Posture**
**Helps Technique** 104
**Brief Anatomy Lesson** 104
**Upper Core Stability** 106
- Shoulder Rows 106
- Shoulder Retractions Letter I 107
- Shoulder Retractions Letter A 107
- Shoulder Retractions Letter T 108
- Shoulder Retractions Letter W 108
- Shoulder External Rotations 109
- Serratus Punch with Lunge 109
- Shoulder Diagonal Pulls 110
- Shoulder Depressions 110
- Scapular Retractions 111

## CHAPTER 6
## CONNECTING YOUR CORE FOR A STRONGER GAME

**Connecting Your Core for a Stronger Game** 114
- Injury Concerns for Golfers 115
- Importance of the Core 116
- Why Connect the Upper & Lower Core? 117
- Benefits of Connect Your Core Stability Training 117
- Warm-Up First 119
**Connect Your Core A** 120
- Supine Bridging & Ball Squeeze
  with Single Arm Diagonal Pull 120
- Supine Bridge & Medicine Ball Arm Raise
  with Stretch Band 121
- Supine Bridging & Single Arm Band Pull
  with Ball Squeeze 121
- Quadruped Bridge & Single Arm Raise
  with Band Resistance 122
- Quadruped Bridge & Resisted Torso Rotations
  on Unstable Base 122
- Split Squat on Ball with Resisted Torso Rotation 123
- Lateral Sit-Ups on Ball 123
- Ball Squats & Shoulder External Rotation 124
- Split Squat & Shoulder Upright Single
  or Double Arm Rows 124
- Squat & Shoulder Forward Press 125
**Connect Your Core B** 126
- Supine Bridging & Ball Squeeze
  with Double Arm Diagonal Pull 126
- Supine Bridge over Physio Ball & Knee Extension 127

# Table of Contents

- Prone Bridge Feet on Ball & Walk Arms Out    127
- Supine Bridge & Medicine Ball Torso Rotation
  with Stretch Band    128
- Split Squat on Ball
  with Straight Arm Torso Rotation    128
- Ball Squats with Ball Squeeze &
  Shoulder External Rotation    129
- Split Squat & Shoulder Press    129
- Split Squat & Shoulder Forward Press    130
- Squat, Ball Squeeze & Shoulder Forward Press    130
- Squat, Ball Squeeze & Lateral Raise
  with Bicep Curl    131
**Connect Your Core C**    132
- Supine Bridge & Hamstring Pull
  with Stretch Band Diagonal Pull    132
- Supine Bridging & Double Arm Band Pull
  with Ball Squeeze    133
- Split Squat on Ball
  with Bent Arm Torso Rotation    133
- Ball Squats with Ball Squeeze &
  Shoulder Diagonal Pull    134
- Split Squat & Shoulder Diagonal Pull    134
- Split Squat & Shoulder Lateral Raise    135
- Split Squat & Torso Rotation    135
- Squat, Ball Squeeze & Shoulder Elevation    136
- Split Squat & Shoulder Forward Press
  with Ball at Side    136
- Squat, Ball Squeeze & Double Arm Diagonal Pull    137
**Connect Your Core D – Knee Stability Focus**    138
- Side Lying Hip Abduction with Ball Squeeze    139
- Supine Bridging & Hamstring Pull    139
- Wall Squats with Ball at Back    140
- Sumo Squats with Ball at Back    140
- Single Leg Squats with Ball at Back    141
- Dynamic Hip Hikes with Ball Pull Down    141
- Dynamic Hip Hikes with Ball at Back    142
- Single Leg 1/4 Squat with Ball at Side    142
- Split Squat & Diagonal Torso Twist with Ball    143
- Split Squat & Shoulder Diagonal Pull    143
**Connect Your Core E – Hip Stability Focus**    144
- Clamshell Hip Abduction    145
- Side Lying Hip Abduction    145
- Side Lying Hip Adduction    146
- Quadruped Bridge & Single Leg Extension
  with Forearms on Ball    146
- Prone Bridge Feet on Ball & Walk Arms Out    147
- Lateral Bridging on Ball    147

- Lateral Bridging on Ball & Leg Lift    148
- Split Squats with Ball at Back    148
- Single Leg Squat & Resisted Shoulder Flexion    149
- Sumo Squat & Double Arm Raise    149

## CHAPTER 7
## MEDICINE BALL DRILLS TO IMPROVE YOUR GAME

**Medicine Ball Drills to Improve Your Game**    152
- General Warm-Up    153
- Medicine Ball Training Program A
  (Alignment Strength & Stability)    154
- Medicine Ball Training Program B
  (Balance Strength & Stability)    155
- Medicine Ball Training Program C
  (Connected Core Strength & Stability)    156

## CHAPTER 8
## CROSS TRAINING FOR GOLFERS

**Cross Training for Golfers (45-55 Minutes Fitness)**    160
- Workout A – 45 Minute Fitness    161
- Workout B – 55 Minute Fitness    163
- Workout C – 55 Minute Fitness    166
**Workout Tips**    169

## CHAPTER 9
## SMART STRETCHING GUIDELINES

**Smart Stretching Guidelines**    172
- Whirlpool stretches    172
- Conform stretching (pre-activity)    173
- Conform stretching (post-training)    173
- Slow, static stretching    176
- Lower body stretches    176
- Upper body stretches    177
- Facilitated partner stretching    177
- Fit to play Golf – Training tips    178
**Rules of Stretching**    179

## CHAPTER 10
## SOFT TISSUE RELEASE WITH SMALL BALL

**Soft Tissue Release
with Small Ball (Muscle and Fasciae)** 182
- Choose the right size ball 183
- Precautions and contraindications 183
- Getting started 184

## CHAPTER 11
## RULES OF RECOVERY FOR GOLFERS

**Rules of Recovery for Golfers** 190
- Rules of Recovery 191
- Re-Hydrate 191
- Re-Fuel 192
- Re-Align the Body 192
- Recovery Work 193
- Release the Soft Tissue 193
- Regain and Maintain Muscle Length 194
- Re-Set the Balance Clock 194
- Re-Connect the Core 195
- Reinvigorate with Hydrotherapy Menu 196
- Resynchronize during Travel 197
**Conclusion** 199

## PUBLISHING INFORMATION

- Publishing information 200
- Production 200
- Photo credits 200
- Selected References 201
**About the Authors** 208

## IMPORTANT CAUTION TO READERS

The contents of this book are not intended to be used as a substitute for medical advice from a qualified professional. All matters regarding your health require proper medical supervision. For specific medical or training advice and treatment, and as a general rule, athletes, coaches and parents should personally consult with a physician or other appropriate healthcare professional before beginning any exercise program, including the ones described in this book. The authors and publisher specifically disclaim any liability or responsibility for loss, injury or damages, personal or otherwise, which are allegedly incurred as a consequence, directly or indirectly, of the use and application of any of the contents of this book.

Fit to Play (TM) is the registered trademark of Fit to Play Int. Inc. Vancouver, Canada.

## EXERCISE DEFINITIONS

 **Reps:** Number of times you do the exercise (repetitions)

 **Sets:** Number of times you repeat the repetitions

 **Tempo:** How fast or slow you do the exercises

- **Example A: 1-4-1 Tempo**
  1 second muscles lengthening / 4 seconds hold /
  1 second muscles shortening
- **Example B: 5-0-5 Tempo**
  5 seconds muscles lengthening / 0 seconds hold /
  5 seconds muscles shortening
- **Example C: 3-0-1 Tempo**
  3 seconds muscles lengthening / 0 second hold /
  1 second muscles shortening

## Chapter 1

**Making Yourself a Better Golfer**

To play better more consistent golf & perform your best on the course you must be Fit to Play™

*Fig. 1.1*

*Dynamic flexibility is needed*

*Fig. 1.2*

*Core stability is needed for tough shots*

# Introduction
# Making Yourself a Better Golfer

Golf is an amazing lifetime sport played all around the world in spectacular settings. Tens of millions of people enjoy playing throughout their lifetime from childhood until well past retirement age. The game brings together and challenges individuals from different social strata's, backgrounds and all walks of life. Players of all ages and abilities play socially or in a competitive environment.

Golf's popularity has led to analysis and research striving for an increased understanding of the physiological demands of the game as well as in equipment innovations. Proper technique and good equipment help build a solid game. But another important and often overlooked component is physical training.

Golf is a sport with demands in many of the principle physical fitness components including flexibility, aerobic stamina, power, strength, speed and skill. With the changing nature and demands of golf fitness training and an increased participation by a wide age range of players we must be pro-active in our training plans to ensure that the needs are met for all of the physical components responsible for performance both on and off the golf course.

If you want to improve your golf skills and on course performance, you must improve the specific physical abilities that make up your golf swing. That means you need to work on your golf-specific suppleness/flexibility, your golf-specific stability and strength and your golf-specific stamina/endurance.

Fig. 1.3
The Art and Science of Training
(Courtesy of Racquet Tech Publishers)

Developing proper training, injury prevention, and recovery habits early and sticking to them will help optimize your performance both on and off the golf course.

Successful golfers require physical ability, technical skill, and mental toughness. Designing programs to ensure optimal golf training and improved performance is both an art and a science, with some trial and error added in (see Fig. 1.3). The science to justify training techniques is rapidly catching up to the art of past, current, and future training.

The high performance training tips in this **Fit to Play™ Golf** book are designed by physiotherapists, coaches, physicians, and other sport medicine and science personnel based on cur-

rent research and numerous years of practical experience working with high performance and recreational golfers as well as athletes from many other sport disciplines.

**DON'T JUST PLAY GOLF TO GET INTO SHAPE; GET INTO PROPER SHAPE TO PLAY GOLF.**

To ensure proper training and practice progressions, to optimize training and performance, and to outsmart your injuries, it is important to look at all of the factors that affect your physical training and on course performance.

Create a list of reasons why you want to get exercise and play golf. Even if your goals are as

Fig. 1.4    Fig. 1.5    Fig. 1.6    Fig. 1.7

*Multidimensional training. Because golf performance is multidimensional, so must be the training. Optimal performance depends on a well-designed and structured program.*

simple as getting fitter, wanting to improve health and lose fat, following the advice in this book will help you play better and continue playing longer. Multidimensional training optimizes performance with a well-designed and structured program. *See Fig. 1.4-1.7*

## Factors affecting training and performance

- Your chronological age (maturity and growth and development considerations)
- Your training age (how many years you have been seriously training)
- Your body type
- Your pre-existing general and specific fitness level
- Your strengths and weakness as identified by your coach, sport physiotherapist or fitness coach
- Your general health status
- The rehabilitation status of any of your past or current injuries
- Your strengths and weaknesses as identified by golf/sport-specific assessments

The **Fit to Play™ Golf** training model uses the concept of 'Interconnecting Gears' to illustrate the importance of different factors in producing optimal golf performance and outsmarting injuries.

Implementation of a training program requires management of many interrelated factors. *See Fig. 1.9*

For the golf performance gear to turn smoothly and efficiently, you must have control of the primary training gears including physical training and practice, skill development, sport psychology and recovery.

Golf performance is your central gear, and all of the other gears have an effect on its movement and ultimately affect it. Some golfers can achieve success with high abilities in certain areas but not others; however, to perform optimally and consistently, all of the gears must be working and turning smoothly and efficiently in order to perform at a high level. Players who are

Fig. 1.8

*Practice both off the mats and the fairway*

talented should ensure correct technique to avoid developing bad habits which will inhibit future progress.

**THE MAIN RESPONSIBILITY FOR YOUR GOLF SPECIFIC TRAINING AND PROGRAM DESIGN RESTS WITH YOU.**

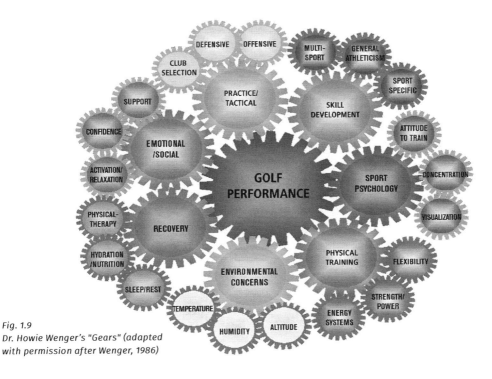

Fig. 1.9
Dr. Howie Wenger's "Gears" (adapted with permission after Wenger, 1986)

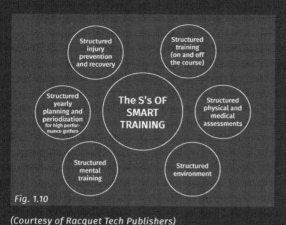

Fig. 1.10

(Courtesy of Racquet Tech Publishers)

Fig. 1.11

Proper club selection

# The S's of Smart Training

The responsibility for making yourself a better golfer falls directly on your shoulders.

You've already purchased the best equipment you can. Now get ready to optimize and improve the most important piece of "equipment" that creates and controls your swing YOU!

To optimize your training and performance, improve recovery, and outsmart your injuries, you need to develop and build a good six-point plan that includes:

**The S's of Smart Training**
(adapted from Petersen & Nittinger, 2006)

1. Structured training (on and off the golf course)

2. Structured physical and medical assessments

3. Structured environment

4. Structured mental training

5. Structured yearly planning and periodization for high performance golfers

6. Structured injury prevention and recovery

Fig. 1.12    Fig. 1.13    Fig. 1.14    Fig. 1.15

Split squats with ball overhead raise to improve leg & shoulder stability.

Structured driving range practice

## S1–STRUCTURED TRAINING
## (ON AND OFF THE GOLF COURSE)

• Develop specific training and tournament plans.

• Consult with a sports physiotherapist, strength and conditioning specialist, or fitness coach.

• Develop contingency plans for adverse weather conditions. Daily physical training adjustment either planned or improvised based on training partners, facilities available, and fatigue level.

• Walk the course whenever possible to boost fitness levels.

• If you're not working with a coach, choose your training partners wisely.

• Find a like-minded training partner with whom you can decide on a training plan and take turns running the practice sessions.

• Organize your training sessions into three parts:
  1. Warm-up
  2. Golf specific drills or exercises
  3. Cool-down and stretching

• Emphasize Quality
  – If the component your training is either aerobic or anaerobic, monitor your intensity by using heart rate, the talk test or rate of perceived exertion to ensure you are working at the right intensity.
  – When strength or stability training, give adequate rest intervals between sets of exercises, try 60 seconds. This ensures that the circulation has time to replenish the local energy (muscle fuel stores) and flush out the waste products produced. Use these rest intervals to stretch or warm up other body parts, as well keep moving to promote removal of waste products in the muscles and decrease the chances of increasing muscle tension or soreness.

Fig. 1.16    Fig. 1.17    Fig. 1.18    Fig. 1.19

*Work on your weakest shots.*

- Minimize Quantity
  - Forget about the 'NO PAIN – NO GAIN' mentality. Training or exercising should not be painful, if it is you are working too hard, failing to rest your body between sessions or wearing the wrong shoes. By emphasizing quality you can decrease the amount you have to do and still get an effective workout in a short time. Go in with a good mindset and get your workout done.

- Exercise Splitting
  - If you can't find 30 minutes per day in one session try splitting it into two 15 minute sessions, or three 10 minute sessions timed for your convenience. This keeps you from skipping the workout. Try the same with your golf range practice if you are pressed for time.

- Work on Your Weaknesses
  - If you are already a strong walker or runner,

try cycling or stair climbing as an alternative. If flexibility is a problem for you ensure adequate time is spent stretching. If stability, strength or balance is your weaknesses then do more strength and stabilization drills.

- Give yourself an honest assessment of your exercise habits, strengths and weaknesses. Your exercise coordinator, physical therapist or trainer can help you identify problem areas and individually design your program.
- When doing any strength work concentrate on the weakest area first and when stretching always begin with the tightest muscle groups. The same holds true for your golf practice. Work on the weakest part of your game at the beginning when you're still fresh.

- Ensure good, sound swing mechanics. Use video analysis and a qualified instructor to optimize

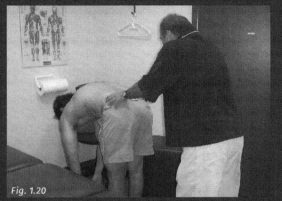 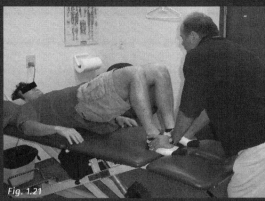

Fig. 1.20    Fig. 1.21

*Structured physical assessment by a qualified professional.*

## S2–STRUCTURED PHYSICAL AND MEDICAL ASSESSMENTS

biomechanics and help identify areas for improvement. This will pay big dividends for your future playing enjoyment and help prevent injuries.

• Include appropriate recovery strategies after each training session.

These assessments will specifically identify physical limitations that may be holding you back from playing your best golf.

### Physical
• Prevention of injuries can be facilitated with preseason screening by a qualified professional. This is very important for those individuals who are new to the game or just starting back at it.

• Screening is best done at least two times per year. Prior to the start of training and 6-8 weeks prior to the start of your heavy tournament/competition period.

• A golf/sport-specific assessment by someone who knows what to look for can save you a lot of pain and frustration later in the season.

Fig. 1.22    Fig. 1.23    Fig. 1.24    Fig. 1.25

*Lower Core & Legs Dynamic Stability Tests*

- Have your physiotherapist/primary health care provider screen you for potential vulnerable or problem areas such as:
  - Previously injured or chronic injury sites.
  - Abnormally tight or loose joints and muscles.
  - Weak or easily fatigued muscles.
  - Postural problems and malalignment issues.

- This preventative assessment is especially important for older players or those with arthritis or other conditions that limit mobility.

- Doing a comprehensive orthopedic assessment including alignment check *(See Fig. 1.20/1.21)* along with some Fit to Play™ – Lower Core & Legs Dynamic Stability Tests like single leg balance, single leg ¼ squat, flat hop and step hop test described in (Petersen & Nittinger, 2006) will give you some ideas as to potential areas that need to be addressed. *See Fig. 1.22 / 1.23 / 1.24 / 1.25*

**Medical**
- Comprehensive pre-participation medical screening including ligament laxity tests, blood work, and urinalysis.

- Get prompt help for any and all injuries and illnesses.

*Fig. 1.26*

*Adequate hydration is important*

*Fig. 1.27*

*Take a penalty stroke to avoid injury.*

## S3-STRUCTURED ENVIRONMENT

In order to train effectively to play your best golf, you must manage all the areas that affect your performance, not just what happens on course. The multifaceted needs of today's competitive golfers cannot be met by the coach or player alone.

As training increases and training demands become more comprehensive and sophisticated, you will need to draw upon the advice and knowledge of other professionals such as physiotherapists, sport physicians, mental trainers, nutritionists, strength and conditioning coaches, and other sport scientists to ensure a safe, effective off- and on-course conditioning program. Optimizing training, on course performance and recovery as well as outsmarting your injuries requires proper management of several factors:

- Adequate hydration and proper nutrition before, during, and after training or tournaments. If unsure speak to a qualified Sports Nutritionist or Dietician. For post play rehydration and re-fueling tips *see page 191-192*.

- Manage jet lag and travel concerns when traveling to and from tournaments. For tips *see page 197-198*.

- Manage environmental concerns such as playing and training in the heat or cold, rain and wind.

- Be sure to use sunscreen and wear a hat and sunglasses when playing. Check your skin monthly for any abnormal changes and see a physician if concerns.

- Be careful ball striking around rocks and exposed roots. Take the unplayable penalty rather than risk injury.

# Making Yourself a Better Golfer

Fig. 1.28
*Ensure you have proper equipment.*

Fig. 1.29
*Mental training can help on & off course performance.*

- At the first sign of lightning, seek shelter or get off the course. It does not matter how well your playing – safety first.

- Get properly equipped with a club fitter from a reputable golf specialty store or pro shop.

- Purchase a pair of good comfortable golf shoes, and make sure they fit. Take your golf socks with you and try on new shoes in the afternoon when feet are a little more swollen.

## S4—STRUCTURED MENTAL TRAINING

- Keep a journal or diary and use it.

- Ensure that resources for appropriate sport psychology are available to you.

- Set goals with your mental trainer or sport psychologist.

- Practice imagery, distraction control, and relaxation techniques.

- Examine your athletic and golfing requirements in the context of your daily life, considering such things as social climate, school, work, family, interpersonal relations, and daily stresses such as exams, deadlines, and personal conflicts.

- Plan well to achieve good balance between on and off course training and relaxation.

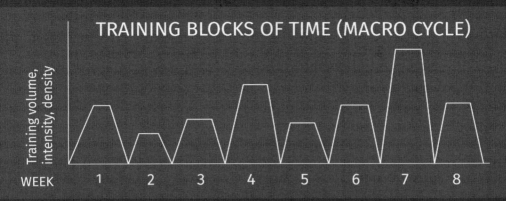

**TRAINING BLOCKS OF TIME (MACRO CYCLE)**

Training volume, intensity, density

WEEK     1     2     3     4     5     6     7     8

*Fig. 1.30*
*Periodization Chart*

- Use video feedback where appropriate to ensure proper swing mechanics and facilitate a mental review of practice without the physical overload to the body's tissues.

- Be patient with yourself both on and off the course. Some days you will be more motivated or have more time than other days. When possible, do more (but don't overdo it). When you can't, do less, or do something different. Train or practice when you feel like doing so, train longer when you have the time and energy.

- Have fun and enjoy yourself. Anxiety and stress in daily life can make you unwell.

- Remember, happy people tend to live longer than miserable ones – and more people may want to invite you to play.

## S5–STRUCTURED YEARLY PLANNING AND PERIODIZATION

- For high performance tournament golfers the yearly planning and periodization of your training season must include pre-competition training, in-competition maintenance, and post season recovery breaks.

- The main objective is to use training blocks to balance the intensity, volume, and density of training competition and recovery. *See Fig. 1.30*

- Your competition season should be planned for playing your best golf at tournaments by dividing training time into three phases:
  1. Pre-competition
     (preparing for a golf tournament).
  2. In-competition maintenance
     (tournament day/week).
  3. Post-competition rest and active rest
     (recovery after a tournament).

- Yearly planning and periodization will reduce

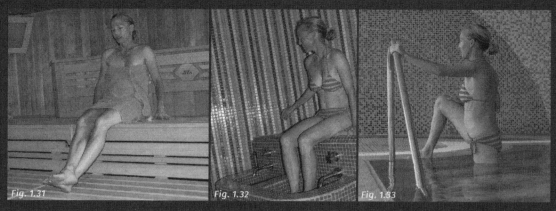

Fig. 1.31    Fig. 1.32    Fig. 1.33

*Recovery. Proper recovery strategies are essential to maximize workout results.*

the risk of boredom, staleness, burnout, over-training, and injury.

- Planning gives the player and coach a better understanding of the overall training program, its goals, and its implementation.

**PROPER PLANNING & PERIODIZATION WILL OPTIMIZE GOLF PERFORMANCE AND DECREASE INJURY POTENTIAL.**

## S6–STRUCTURED INJURY PREVENTION AND RECOVERY

Injury prevention and management must be an integral part of your on and off course training program. There are several key components to successfully out-smart your injuries.

### Proper Training and Recovery Strategies

Training and playing are never 100-percent injury free. You work hard, pushing your limits to achieve your best performance, and injuries can occur. Due to the asymmetric (one sided) nature of golf the most common injuries are of the overuse variety. The cumulative effect of numerous swings pounding out drives on the range and the repetitive actions during off course training like running, jumping and lifting weights can cause tissue breakdown and inflammation (micro-trauma).

Injury prevention is an important part of the training plan of every golfer. Injuries can be minimized and controlled with proper recovery

Fig. 1.34    Fig. 1.35

*Ensure proper club carrying and lifting ergonomics to avoid back problems.*

strategies and a sensible injury prevention and management strategy at the heart of your training plan. The benefits of structured recovery sessions are well documented, both in terms of improved performance and decreased injury rates. *See page 188-199.*

The best planned and periodized training program is of little use if you are always injured and unable to train or play golf effectively. Ensure proper recovery strategies are followed. *See Fig. 1.31 / 1.32 / 1.33*

Learn proper lifting techniques to avoid getting injured while lifting and transporting your golf bag and pull cart to and from the car.

Use a pull cart to reduce back stress and strain. Players with back concerns should try pushing the cart with alternating arms.

If carrying your clubs try using a double strap type golf bag to reduce one sided pressure on the upper core and shoulders and lower core and legs. *See Fig. 1.34*

Listen to your body. Seek appropriate treatment for pains that don't go away. Pay particular attention to fatigue, pain or aching in the back, hips and shoulder region. *See Fig. 1.35*

## Chapter 2

**The ABCs of Smart Training for Golfers**

Improve skills faster & increase training with the ABC's of Smart Training for Golfers.

Fig. 2.1

*Actively and passively stretch tight muscles with small ball release.*

Fig. 2.2

*Actively strengthen and stabilize muscles that are weak.*

# The ABCs of Smart Training for Golfers

When designing your golf specific training program, it will help to follow the concepts outlined in this section. Apply the ABCs of smart golf training during all off- and on-the course training, other sports and daily activities.

This will increase training potential, help improve golf skills faster, shorten recovery time and decrease the potential for injury.

## A1–ATHLETIC STANCE AND ALIGNMENT

Proper athletic stance means being prepared for the training activity ahead. Think of keeping the knees soft (slightly bent), switch on your core (pelvic tension like a dimmer switch), and keep your shoulders relaxed and down and head neutral. Correct anatomical alignment must be attained and maintained to allow for proper force distribution on the weight-bearing structures during playing and training activities. Relaxed muscles are fluid and can move faster creating more acceleration. Tight muscles will slow you down and restrict your range of motion.

This can be facilitated by:
- Actively and passively stretching muscles that are usually short and stiff (e.g., hamstrings, hip flexors, calves, and pectorals). *See Fig. 2.1*
- Actively strengthening muscles that are usually long and weak (e.g., lower abdominals, upper back and posterior shoulder girdle muscles [infraspinatus], and hip external rotators [gluteal muscles]). *See Fig. 2.2*

Fig. 2.3   Fig. 2.4

Train with a proper athletic stance and alignment.

Fig. 2.5

Proper alignment is important for an athletic golf posture.

Proper alignment starts with excellent spinal alignment. To align your spine:
- Imagine someone pulling you by the top of your head, lengthening out your spine.
- The neck should be long and the shoulders relaxed, back, and down.

Checks on proper alignment include these:
- During movement emphasize correct knee alignment, with knees always tracking over the toes but not going past them.
- When doing lunges or split squats, keep the line of gravity through the pubic bone of the pelvis to avoid shear forces on the pelvic joints. *See Fig. 2.3/2.4*
- In the golf setup the nose, sternum (chest bone) and spine should all be aligned. *See Fig 2.5*

**Athletic Golf Posture**
To assume an athletic position for the golf swing start by standing tall, feet comfortably wide apart without a club in your hands. Tuck your thumbs into your belt or belt loops and push down in to your hips loading your upper legs with a slight bend in the knee so you feel stable. Now let go of your belt and let your arms hang naturally.

Relaxed muscles are fluid and can move faster. Tight muscles will slow you down and restrict your range of motion

Having a wider stance creates a more solid base of support allowing a little harder swing with more control.

*Fig. 2.6*

*Challenge your body with different exercises.*

*Fig. 2.7*

*New challenges lead to adaptive change.*

## A2—ADAPTIVE TRAINING

High performance and superior levels of golf fitness are the result of many months or years of well-planned training. Adaptations occur to the body's systems when they are challenged by new stresses. If the workload is not high enough, no adaptation will occur. If the workload is too high, mal-adaptation occurs, possibly leading to over-training, overuse, and injury. The following are some principles of adaptive training:

- When designing a training program, one must respect the time frames for anatomical, physiological, and psychological adaptation to occur.

- Regular participation—at least 2–4 days per week—in a planned activity outside of golfing.

- Overload:
  - The training load must be high enough to tax the body's systems during a training session.
  - Overload encourages physical change and promotes adaptation.
  - To achieve overload, the duration of the activity must be long enough to produce a training effect and the intensity of the workouts must increase in a gradual and progressive manner.
  - A good rule of thumb is to gradually increase volume or intensity 10 percent per week.

- Regularly scheduling rest or recovery days (at least one per week):
  - Helps tissues such as muscle, tendon, ligament, and bone to adapt to the new stresses being placed on them through physical training and hitting balls.
  - Helps prevent staleness or over-training.

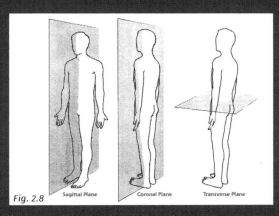

Fig. 2.8    Sagittal Plane    Coronal Plane    Transverse Plane

*(Courtesy of Racquet Tech Publishers)*

Fig. 2.9

*Challenge balance by standing on balance pods and bouncing 2 different balls.*

## B1–BALANCE EXERCISES

As physical therapists and fitness coaches we have long known the benefits of balance and body awareness exercises in rehabilitating injuries and in sport specific training. Balance exercises can improve the biomechanics of your golf swing in many ways. Proper balance enables the neuromuscular system to dynamically stabilize the entire kinetic chain in all 3 planes of motion. *See Fig. 2.8.* This is important throughout the full swing motion from address to takeaway and backswing to the top and into downswing to impact and release, follow through and finish.

Balance exercises are a fundamental component of functional mobility and dynamic activity and should be a part of every golfer's training routine. Working on balance training is even more important as you increase strength, stability and power because you want to continually reset the balance clock and have the opportunity to practice and play with your newly adapted and strengthened muscles.

**Balance exercises**

• Avoid problems associated with playing a 'one-sided' sport by doing balance exercises equally on right and left sides. *See Fig. 2.9*

• Work on joint sense (proprioception).

• Reset the balance clock with a variety of exercises. *See Fig. 2.10 / 2.11*

• Stimulate the complex interactions of the neuromuscular system when incorporated with closed chain and functional exercises.

• Are especially important after injury where there is any joint swelling and decreased proprioception.

• Should be included as part of the daily training plan as the golf swing depends on an element of coordinated balance in many planes of movement.

Fig. 2.10    Fig. 2.11    Fig. 2.12

*Challenge balance with single leg stance drills.*

*Improve balance by practicing some short shots balancing on one leg.*

### Balanced Controlled Swing

Balance exercises can help improve your golf swing by maintaining proper joint alignment helping control the swing. A swing that is out of control is an ugly swing to watch. Optimum balance enables the muscles and nerves to work together to dynamically stabilize the kinetic chain in all 3 planes of motion while producing speed and power during the swing. If balance is lacking the ability to execute a proper rhythmical golf swing will be compromised. Consistent long ball hitters all have great balance. *See Fig. 2.10/2.11*

Help improve lower core and leg stability by hitting a 6 or 7 iron with feet and knees together without losing your balance. Place ball in line with middle of feet and make a full swing and follow through maintaining a balanced position. As well try hitting some short shots while balancing on one leg. *See Fig. 2.11*

### Balance Your Life

Avoid becoming one-dimensional in your professional or personal life. You must have balance to be successful in your social life, workplace and in becoming a better golfer. Keep perspective on what things are really important and success will follow both on and off the course.

| In gerneral, training the different components of fitness can be done as follows: | |
| --- | --- |
| Suppleness (flexibility) | 4 - 6 x per week |
| Stamina (aerobic) | 3 - 6 x per week |
| Stamina (anaerobic) | 1 - 2 x per week |
| Strength & Stability | 2 - 3 x per week |
| Skill (golf & other) | 2 - 6 x per week |
| Power & Speed Work | 1 - 2 x per week |
| | |

*Table 2.1*
*Suggested frequency of exercise sessions by type*

## B2–BALANCED TRAINING PROGRAMS

Balanced training means a correct ratio of time spent on the different components of fitness and performance: flexibility, stamina (aerobic and anaerobic), strength, speed, coordination, and golf-specific skill exercises. All are important components of fitness and should be included in your program, depending on the phase of training you are in. Obviously, different activities have different demands and will require more emphasis on one type of training than another.

### Example
Each training week or cycle should include the proper amount of rest or alternative activity to allow for adequate adaptation to occur. Training-to-rest ratios vary depending upon the energy systems used, the event or sport, and the personality and training age of the athlete.

## C1–CONSISTENT TRAINING

Training should be consistent enough to force adaptations to the cardio-respiratory system (heart and lungs) and the musculo-skeletal system (soft tissue and bone). *Table 2.1* gives guidelines for the necessary training consistency to induce the desired adaptations.

**Consistent training means:**
- Knowing what you are doing and working with professionals.
- Having confidence in your training program and plans.
- Having confidence in both on- and off-course training plans.
- Being able to justify what you are doing and why you are doing it based on research and experience.

Fig. 2.13

*Supine bridging*

Fig. 2.14

*Connect your core adding balls and bands.*

You will want to continually individualize your program based on your needs and you will progress your training based on fitness gains, goals, and feed-back from your golf coach/pro, therapists, and strength and conditioning coaches.

Consistency is one antidote to the principle of reversibility: If you don't use it, you'll lose it. The training effect will be lost if training is stopped or spaced too far apart to trigger the adaptations.

## C2–CONNECT YOUR CORE

In golf you must train to improve the body's ability to stabilize the core and generate power outward to the limbs as you swing the club.

- Connected core musculature helps create movement at the spine and also exerts a stabilizing muscular force to maintain a neutral spine and pelvis.

- Use a variety of movements and training types to ensure a balanced approach to core training.

- Always switch on your core – like a dimmer switch of a light (low background tension in the pelvic floor and lower abdominals) during all exercise and activity (Petersen & Sirdevan, 2006) including golfing, training, and playing other sports.

- 3-Dimensional core stability is important to give you the strong platform to execute movements with the extremities, especially the legs.
- Many commonly prescribed exercises are machine based and isolate a single joint in one plane of motion. This does not allow for the rotation, torque and angular movement of the kinetic chain needed in a full golf swing.

- Normally the lower abdominals switch on or fire in pre-anticipation of any movement but with dysfunction there is a timing delay and studies have

Fig. 2.15    Fig. 2.16    Fig. 2.17    Fig. 2.18

*Squats with elastic band resistance.*    *Split squats with torso rotation and elastic band resistance.*

shown that without efficient and optimal recruitment, subsequent spinal dysfunction can occur.

- Remember, efficient movement needs optimal stabilization and requires intact bones, joints, and ligaments; efficient and coordinated muscle action; and appropriate neural responses.

- Supine bridging *(see Fig. 2.13)*: This core exercise allows you to gain control of the pelvic floor and lower abdominal (transversus abdominus).

- Adding balls and bands to create instability and add resistance helps to connect your core. *See Fig. 2.14*

Squats with stretch/resistance band pulls and a ball squeeze (see fig. 2.15/2.16) and split squats with band resistance and rotation *(see Fig. 2.17/ 2.18)* help connect the upper and lower core.

See "Connecting Your Core for a Stronger Game" from page 112-149 for more training ideas.

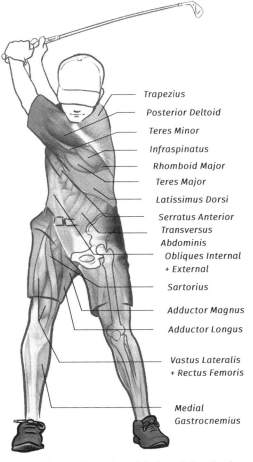

Trapezius
Posterior Deltoid
Teres Minor
Infraspinatus
Rhomboid Major
Teres Major
Latissimus Dorsi
Serratus Anterior
Transversus Abdominis
Obliques Internal + External
Sartorius
Adductor Magnus
Adductor Longus
Vastus Lateralis + Rectus Femoris
Medial Gastrocnemius

*Some of the muscles activated during a full golf swing.*

Fig. 2.19    Fig. 2.20

Split squats raising a ball above head is a closed chain exercise for the hip, knee & ankle.

Fig. 2.21

Hamstring leg curls. Open chain exercise.

## C3—CHAIN EXERCISES: CLOSED, PARTIALLY CLOSED, AND OPEN

To understand the concepts surrounding closed, partially closed, and open kinetic chain, view your body as a length of chain. A closed-kinetic chain activity is defined as an activity in which the terminal joint meets considerable external resistance which prohibits or restrains free motion; whereas, an open-kinetic chain activity is defined as an activity in which the terminal joint is free (Steindler, 1955).

Closed kinetic chain exercise occurs when the hands or feet support the body weight. Closed kinetic chain is best referred to as dynamic and functional with the whole body working as an integrated unit. Closed-kinetic chain activities may help improve dynamic stability through joint approximation and co-contraction (Goldbeck & Davies, 2000). Examples of this would be a lunge or a squat. *See Fig. 2.19 / 2.20*

Open kinetic chain exercise occurs when the end of the chain (arms or legs) is not fixed and does not support the weight of the body. Open kinetic chain exercises are best characterized as isolation movements—for instance, leg extension, leg curls, or bicep curls. *See Fig. 2.21*

Partially closed chain exercises would be any that partially support your body weight and require an integrated response from the muscles of the body. Examples of this would be a push-up position where the hands and feet partially bear the weight or any activity that loads resistance through the hands and arms and into the torso, as when using resistance bands.

An example would be split squats, lunges or step ups with elastic band resistance. *See Fig. 2.22/2.23.* The step up is a closed chain exercises and the resistance bands have the arms and shoulders working in a partially closed chain manner.

Fig. 2.22     Fig. 2.23

*Step-ups. Train in a hip-extended position of function while partially closing the kinetic chain and working the upper core and arms.*

Fig. 2.24     Fig. 2.25

*Dynamic hip hikes work the anterior oblique sling. With the correct equipment these exercises can be done inside or outside.*

In ground-based sports such as golf, all of the body movements work within a kinetic chain linkage from the ground up through the trunk to the upper core and arms.

Utilizing closed and partially closed chain exercises with varied band and ball resistance will increase stability of the different muscle slings. This will help improve the golfer's ability to control the backswing, accelerate the downswing and decelerate the finish.

Exercises should be performed with the following points in mind:

- Exercises should be done in a controlled, coordinated, and functional manner.

- Exercises should work the hip in an extended position because it is the position of activity and function *(see Fig. 2.22 / 2.23 / 2.24 / 2.25 and Fig. 2.31/2.32/2.33).*

- Exercises like step-ups, split squats, and lunges can be made more functional by adding elastic tubing to partially close the upper core chain.

- Activation of the kinetic chain sling patterns from the legs through the hips and back to the shoulder restores the force-dependent motor activation pattern and normal biomechanical positions.

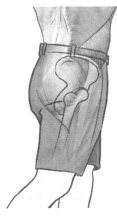

*Extended hip position at finish of a swing.*

Fig. 2.26      Fig. 2.27      Fig. 2.28      Fig. 2.29

*Using different pieces of equipment like balls and resistance bands will help add a balance component and diversify your workouts.*

## D1–DIVERSITY IN DRILLS AND TRAINING

Training with diversity means using a variety of methods in your weekly program. For example, aerobic training may use a mix of running, cycling, swimming, or in-line skating to get the desired effect of aerobic fitness.

Besides offering a greater range of non-weight-bearing alternatives for training, diverse training promotes development of fundamental skills. For example, core training may use a mix of floor, seated, standing, squatting and lunging exercises using balls and stretch bands/cords. *See Fig. 2.26 / 2.27 / 2.28 / 2.29*

- Altering exercises.

- Altering the sequence of exercises.

- Changing the tempo to avoid drudgery and avoid over-training.

- Adding weights, balance equipment, balls, and stretch cords to increase the core component. *See Fig. 2.26 / 2.27 / 2.28 / 2.29*

- Have specific training goals that make sense and have appropriate application to golf.

**Diversify training by:**

- Analyzing the sport-specific movements and adding movement and challenging balance in ways that mimic the activity without introducing a high element of risk for injury.

Never do the same workout program for more than six to eight weeks. Regularly change things up to activate different muscle groups and patterns of movement.

Fig. 2.30

Fig. 2.31

Fig. 2.32

Fig. 2.33

*Many shots are played from a hip extended position.*

*Hip extension. Strength and stability in this position is crucial to optimize functional movement.*

## D2–DYNAMIC HIP EXTENSION EXERCISES

- Hip-extended strength is the position of function for most sports including golf. *See Fig. 2.30*

- The competitive posture shortens anterior muscles so athletes must have strength and stability into hip extension. *See Fig. 2.31/ 2.32/2.33*

- Training should include exercises that promote dynamic flexibility, stability and strength.

- This type of exercise improves general fitness and helps you in your normal activities of daily living, such as lifting, stepping, carrying, pushing, or pulling.

- Utilize exercises that focus on connecting the core to the activity and that combine upper body, lower body, and core moves.

## E1–EXERCISE AT A SLOW AND CONTROLLED TEMPO (SOMETIMES)

- Some exercises should be performed slowly. Controlled repetitions that take three to four seconds to complete help increase tension in the muscle fibers and build strength without too much stress on the soft tissues.

- Avoid using momentum to perform an exercise or doing exercises that are uncontrolled.

- Remember, training is not necessarily golfing. Don't confuse the two when doing every exercise.

**DON'T JUST GOLF TO GET FIT, GET FIT TO PLAY™ GOLF.**

# The ABCs of Smart Training for Golfers

*Functional training like this twisting step up and medicine ball throw develops powerful and coordinated multi-joint and multi-dimensional movement.*

## E2–EXCELLENT FORM

While training, attention must be paid to form:

- Exercises should be functional and mimic golf specific challenges and movements.

- Always remember the importance of good form when doing an exercise.

- Correct form includes proper breathing, exhale on exertion (no breath holding), and always switch on your core (pelvic tension) prior to any exercise.

- Ensure quality of motion using good bio-mechanics as opposed to quantity with less precise form.

## F1–FUNCTIONAL TRAINING

Functional movement requires all the joints in the kinetic chain and the neurological system to work in concert in a coordinated and harmonious manner. *See Fig. 2.34 / 2.35*

**Tips for functional training**

- Use multi-dimensional, multi-joint movement, not just isolated actions at one joint.

- Start by practicing parts of the movement, then combine the parts into movement drills, then practice and rehearse the movement drills, and then incorporate it into the activity or sport.

- Integrate multiple joint movements, linking the closed and partially closed kinetic chain.

- Functional training does not isolate muscles in a single plane of movement, but instead requires stabilization in three planes of motion during dynamic movement.

Fig. 2.36

*Adapt to different venues of training.*

# Keep it fun!

Training should be **fun AND stimulating**, both **physically AND mentally**.

If it's not, why are you doing it?

- Functional training must be dynamic in nature and require the participant to accelerate, decelerate, stop on a dime, change directions, react to ground forces, and constantly adjust and react to different situations.

- Effective function and rehabilitation are best developed by using a variety of methods.

- Choose exercises that are functional in nature and reflect the current research on how our muscles and fascial tissue kinetically link together to form sling systems connecting the lower core and legs through the torso to upper core and arms.

## F2–FLEXIBLE AND FUN PLANNING

- Remain flexible in your planning; training plans can be modified based on situation and circumstance.

- Be in control of your training plan, not a slave to it.

- When traveling, equipment and facilities will vary greatly. Be flexible and adaptable in your training routines. *See Fig. 2.36*

- Take advantage of good training facilities, including whirlpools and other recovery tools, when available, and have other routines you can do with minimal equipment when travelling.

- Training for golf and doing different drills are, by their very nature, fun.

- Improvement is fun. Challenge yourself with hard training that makes use of natural movement patterns and allows you to improve and optimize performance.

- Remember that you train for golf and compete to achieve success, but also to be with friends and have fun.

## Chapter 3

**Dynamic Warm-Up & Cool-Down Guidelines**

*Optimize your training time and prevent injuries with a proper dynamic warm up and cool down.*

*General warm-up of the large muscles with different activities.*

# Dynamic Warm-Up & Cool-Down Guidelines

Whether you're training to get ready for golf season or warming up for a cross training session following the advice below will help you through a dynamic warm-up and ensure perform better. You should do a sport- or activity-specific warm-up before every training session. Optimize your training time and get the most for your time and energy, by being both physically and mentally prepared before starting an activity.

Slowly warming-up the body helps prevent injuries caused by going too hard and too fast with cold, unlubricated muscles and joints. Dynamic warm-up is the activity of choice before activity. Warm-ups vary depending on the type, duration, and intensity of activity you are going to do. It consists of a group of exercises performed immediately before the activity and provides a period of adjustment from rest to exercise. Recent research indicates that pre-activity overall warm-up may contribute to

a reduction in injury while purely static stretching does not.

You must warm up to train, golf or stretch. Use any large muscle group activities like running, elliptical trainer, cycling, rowing, or skipping rope until a light sweat is achieved. This ensures that the temperature of the joints and soft tissues is increased. A good 10–15 minute warm-up will help optimize your training time. For individuals that are new to exercises doing a prolonged warm up for 20–30 minutes will help contribute to your general conditioning, especially early in the season. *See Fig. 3.1 / 3.2 / 3.3*

- Start slowly and increase the intensity and complexity of the warm-up.
- Take extra time to perform a good warm-up on cold or windy days. A warm muscle is not only stronger, but its elastic properties are also increased (a two-degree increase of muscle temperature is thought to increase a

| Borg Scale of Perceived Exertion | | Talk Test Guidelines |
| --- | --- | --- |
| 0 | Nothing at all | |
| 1 | Very easy | Can very easily carry on a conversation |
| 2 | Easy | |
| 3 | Moderate | |
| 4 | Somewhat Hard | You should be able to carry on a conversation |
| 5 | Hard | |
| 6 | | Cannot talk continuously |
| 7 | Very Hard | |
| 8 | | |
| 9 | | Cannot talk at all |
| 10 | Very, Very Heavy (Maximal) | |

*Dynamic Warm-up Intensity*
*Borg Scale of Perceived Exertion Talk Test Guidelines (Borg, 1982)*

muscle's elastic properties by as much as 15–20 percent), allowing for better shock absorption.

- Warm up until you have a light (sweat) glow or damp armpits helps achieve this.
- Use activity specific movements to help improve the relaxation-contraction coordination of the joints' prime movers and stabilizers. This will lead to more efficient movement and improved performance.

Whatever warm-up methods you use, your intensity should not be so hard that you are creating lactic acid in the muscles. So keep your heart rate low – about 110–130, depending on your age and maximum heart rate and also don't go too hard or too intensely for more that 1-15 seconds. On the Borg Scale of Perceived Exertion you will be working between levels 3 and 5 *(See diagram at top of page).*

**A Dynamic Warm-Up Should Include:**

1) General (aerobic) Knee Warm Up
2) Balance Warm Up
3) Lower Core and Leg Warm Up
4) Upper Core and Arm Warm Up
5) CNS (central nervous system) Warm Up
6) Muscle Tendon Warm Up

**YOU SHOULD DO A SPECIFIC DYNAMIC WARM-UP BEFORE EVERY TRAINING OR GOLF PRACTICE SESSION TO PREPARE YOURSELF BOTH MENTALLY AND PHYSICALLY.**

Fig. 3.4

*Skipping is a good general warm-up before training.*

Fig. 3.5  Fig. 3.6

*Assisted squats*

Fig. 3.7  Fig. 3.8

*Leg swings (front-to-back)*

# Sample Dynamic Warm-Up

## W1–GENERAL (AEROBIC) & KNEE WARM UP

If you have time and access to a gym get on the treadmill, elliptical trainer, exercise bike, stair-climber or rowing machine for 5-15 minutes. If that is not an option, do some easy jogging or take a skipping rope with you and use it for several minutes. *See Fig. 3.4*

Do these warm-up exercises before any weights or any exercise (running, jumps, sports) that involves knee flexion (bending). These assisted squat exercises help lubricate the under surface of the knee cap (patella), so it slides smoothly and tracks properly. Do 2 sets of 10 repetitions *See Fig. 3.5 / 3.6*

Fig. 3.9  Fig. 3.10  Fig. 3.11  Fig. 3.12

Leg swings side to side open up the hips.

Leg swings (figure of 8) switches on the core, challenges balance and loosens the hips.

Fig. 3.13  Fig. 3.14  Fig. 3.15  Fig. 3.16

Cross over drills focus on athletic posture.

Warm up hips with these high knees drills.

High heels butt kicks

Side shuffle drills keeping hands out in front.

## W2–BALANCE & LEG WARM-UP

Hang onto your golf club, a fence, tree or wall and further warm-up the lower core and challenge balance reactions with leg swings front and back, side to side and figure of 8's. Do 2 sets of 10 repetitions.

*See Fig. 3.7 / 3.8 / 3.9 / 3.10 / 3.11 / 3.12*

## W3–LOWER CORE & LEG WARM-UP

As you jog around add in some crossovers, high knees, high heels, skipping, and side shuffle steps to improve coordination and add to the warm-up. Stand tall and switch on your core (like a dimmer switch on a light) while doing these exercises. Try doing 2-4 repetitions of 5 to 10 meters of each.

*See Fig. 3.13 / 3.14 / 3.15 / 3.16*

Fig. 3.17    Fig. 3.18    Fig. 3.19    Fig. 3.20

*Hurdlers high knees bring your knee up to hip height, first inside, then straight in front and then outside.*

Fig. 3.21    Fig. 3.22    Fig. 3.23    Fig. 3.24

*Thread the needle*      *Torso twists*

Try some hurdlers high knees challenging your balance and warming up the hip. Bring your knee up to the inside then back down and up straight and back down then up and outside and back down. Minimize ground contact and try 3-5 repetitions of each movement
*See Fig. 3.17 / 3.18 / 3.19 / 3.20*

## W4–UPPER CORE & SHOULDER WARM-UP

Proper warm-up prepares the muscles you will use in training and prepares the joints for movement and dynamic stability throughout a full range of motion. Activity specific movements help to improve the relaxation-contraction coordination of the joints' prime movers and stabilizers leading to more efficient movement and performance.

Fig. 3.25

Arm swing circles

Fig. 3.26

Arm swings front and back

Fig. 3.27

Arm swings in figure of 8 pattern

Fig. 3.28    Fig. 3.29

Stand tall and pump arms and legs in a sprinters motion.

Try doing 2 sets of 10 repetitions of thread the needle, torso twists and arm swings forward and back and in circles and in a figure of eight motion. These warm-ups will help to get the thoracic spine moving into rotation and improve correct muscle firing sequence, as well as stabilize the shoulder girdle.

See Fig. 3.21 / 3.22 / 3.23 / 3.24 / 3.25 / 3.26 / 3.27

## W5–CNS (CENTRAL NERVOUS SYSTEM)

Here is a speed warm up you can do in limited space on the side of the gym or playing field that will help trigger your central nervous system (CNS). Do a sprinters motion running on the spot "sewing machines" for 2 x 6–8 seconds at a medium tempo (60 % of full speed). Follow these with 2–3 x "sewing machine accelerations" where you gradually accelerate up to 80% of your full speed at the 6-8 second mark. See Fig. 3.28 / 3.29

*Fig. 3.31*     *Fig. 3.32*

*Alternating lunges. Keep knees over toes and increase depth of lunge slowly.*

*Fig. 3.30*

*Ricochet jumps. Stand tall & have short ground contact.*

## W6–MUSCLE TENDON WARM-UP

You need to warm up the muscles and tendons as well. One of the best ways of doing this is to combine ricochet jumps and alternating lunges. Alternating Lunges are done in place. Gradually increase depth of lunge (don't go past 90 degrees), keep knee lined up over toes. Try 2-3 sets of 10 reps.

*See Fig. 3.30 / 3.31 / 3.32*

**Ricochet jumps are done in place as follows:**
- 2 x 20 jumps at personal rhythm
- 2 x 20 as fast as possible (short ground contact)

# Quick Sample Warm-Ups

## WARM-UP A

**1) General (aerobic) Knee Warm Up**
- Cycle/Treadmill run x 5-15 minutes
- Assisted squats 2 x 5-10-15

**2) Balance Warm Up**
- Leg swings (front & back) 2 x 10
- Legs swings (side to side) 2 x 10

**3) Lower Core and Leg Warm Up**
- Side shuffles 2 x 5–10 meters
- Skips 2 x 5–10 meters

**4) Upper Core and Arm Warm Up**
- Thread the needle 2 x 10

**5) CNS (central nervous system) Warm Up**
- Sewing machine accelerations 2 x 6-8 seconds

**6) Muscle Tendon Warm Up**
- Ricochet Jumps (personal rhythm 3 x 20)
- Alternating lunges 2 x 5

## WARM-UP B

**1) General (aerobic) Knee Warm Up**
- Jog/Elliptical/Stair climber x 5-15 minutes
- Assisted squats 2 x 5-10-15

**2) Balance Warm Up**
- Leg swings (front & back + side to side) 1 x 10.

**3) Lower Core and Leg Warm Up**
- Crossovers 2 x 5–10 meters
- High heels 2 x 5–10 meters

**4) Upper Core and Arm Warm Up**
- Arm swings (front & back, side to side) 2 x 10

**5) CNS (central nervous system) Warm Up**
- Sewing machine accelerations 2 x 6-8 seconds

**6) Muscle Tendon Warm Up**
- Alternating lunges 2 x 15

## WARM-UP C

**1) General (aerobic) Knee Warm Up**
- Elliptical / row x 5-15 minutes
- Assisted squats 2 x 5-10-15

**2) Balance Warm Up**
- Leg swings (front and back) 2 x 10
- Leg swings (side to side) 2 x 10

**3) Lower Core and Leg Warm Up**
- Skipping 2 x 5–10 meters
- High Knees 2 x 5–10 meters

**4) Upper Core and Arm Warm Up**
- Torso twists 3 x 10

**5) CNS (central nervous system) Warm Up**
- Sewing machine accelerations 2 x 6-8 seconds

**6) Muscle Tendon Warm Up**
- Ricochets 2 x 10 (as fast as possible)
- Alternating lunges 2 x 10

**NOW YOU'RE READY TO TRAIN OR PLAY SPORTS.**

Fig. 3.33

Hip flexor stretch

Fig. 3.34

Standing quadriceps stretch

Fig. 3.35

Seated gluteal (buttock) stretch

Fig. 3.36

Anterior shoulder (pectoral) stretch

Fig. 3.37

Posterior shoulder stretch

# Cool-Down & Post-Training Conform Stretching

Light stretching after training is important to minimize delayed onset muscle soreness and reduce the potential for injury. Instead of aggressively stretching, do a conform stretch, taking the stretch to the point of light tension and hold for 15-20 seconds (see Chapter 9 pages 170-179). Research indicates that stretches prior to exercise did not prevent lower extremity overuse injuries, but additional static stretches after training and before bed resulted in 50 percent fewer injuries (Hartig and Henderson, 1999). Therefore save the static stretching for after the training session and during the recovery protocol (see Chapter 11 pages 188-199).

Try holding each stretch for 30 seconds and repeat 2-3 times. *See Fig. 3.33 / 3.34 / 3.35 / 3.36 / 3.37 / 3.38 / 3.39 / 3.40 / 3.41*

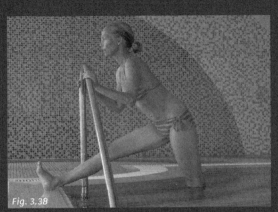

*Fig. 3.38*

*Standing hamstring (posterior thigh) stretch*

*Fig. 3.39*

*Seated hamstring stretch*

*Fig. 3.40*

*Standing adductor (inner thigh) stretch*

*Fig. 3.41*

*Forearm and wrist flexor stretch*

Be systematic, stretching all major muscle groups. This includes leg muscles of the quadriceps, hamstrings, calf, back, abductors, and adductors. Exhale on the initial stretch and then breathe normally. By stretching in the whirlpool or sauna you are giving the muscles, tendons and fasciae tissue a passive external warm-up to assist the stretch.

GO EASY IMMEDIATELY AFTER TRAINING. NOW IS NOT THE TIME TO TRY TO AGGRESSIVELY STRETCH TIGHT, TENSE, MUSCLES.

## Chapter 4

**On Course Golf Specific Warm-Up**

# Warm up to golf, don't just golf to warm up

Fig. 4.1

*Assisted squats warm-up and lubricate the joints.*

# On Course Golf Specific Warm-Up

## GENERAL WARM-UP

Some form of general warm-up should be done before making a single swing. Start with your walk from the car or home to the course. If you have access to an exercise room, get on the exercise bike, stair-climber or rowing machine for a few minutes. Slowly but methodically warming the body's tissues helps prevent injuries that may be caused by swinging too hard, too fast, too soon with cold, un-lubricated muscles and joints. Whether you're getting prepared to hit some balls on the driving range or getting ready for a round of golf, following the advice below will help you optimize your time spent.

## BE PREPARED

Warm up to golf, don't just golf to warm up. To optimize your on course play and get the most for your time and energy, ensure that you are both physically and mentally prepared before heading onto the course. One of the main contributors to injury in the recreational golfer is the complete absence of any pre-golf warm-up routine.

- Proper warm-up prepares the muscles you will use in training and prepares the joints for movement and stability throughout a full range of motion.

- Intense exercise done without a dynamic warm-up has the potential for injury.

- Start slowly and increase the intensity and complexity of the warm-up.

Fig. 4.2

*Different leg swings switch on the core, challenge balance and open the hips.*

- Use swing specific movements to **help improve** the relaxation-contraction coordination of the joints' prime movers and stabilizers leading to more efficient movement and **performance.**

- On colder or windy days it is vital **that you take** the extra time to perform a **good warm-up** because a warm muscle is not **only stronger** but the elastic properties of it **are increased** allowing for better shock absorption.

- A two degree increase of muscle **temperature** is believed to give an increase in **elastic prop-**erties of the muscle by as **much as 15-20%** helping to improve performance **and prevent** muscle strains. Warming-up until **you have a** light (sweat) glow or damp armpits **helps** achieve this.

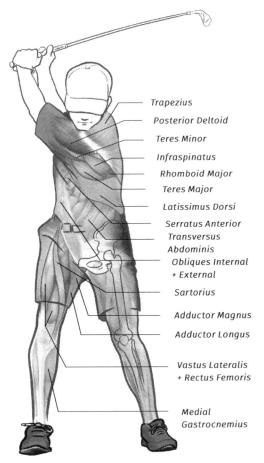

Trapezius
Posterior Deltoid
Teres Minor
Infraspinatus
Rhomboid Major
Teres Major
Latissimus Dorsi
Serratus Anterior
Transversus
Abdominis
Obliques Internal
+ External
Sartorius
Adductor Magnus
Adductor Longus
Vastus Lateralis
+ Rectus Femoris
Medial
Gastrocnemius

*Protect against injury and improve performance by dynamically warming up all of the muscles involved in playing golf.*

# General warm-up

- 5 minutes rope skipping or jogging

🕐 5 minutes

---

# Knee bends

- Bend your knees while holding your arms over your head
- Pull the arms back and stand up straight
- Return to the starting position
- Perform the exercise slowly

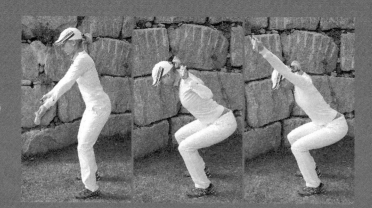

↺ 10

---

# Lunges with extended arms

- Weight on the back leg, the front leg is stretched out
- Weight on your front leg, stretch out the back leg and both arms
- Keep your back straight

↺ 10/10

# Standing scales

- Stand on one leg, pull one knee up, holding your arms out in front of your body
- Lean forward, stretch out your arms and legs

 10/10

# Leg swings

**a) forward and back**
**b) side to side (right-left)**

- Stand on one leg, stretch your arms forward
- Do 1-2 sets of 10 with leg swinging forward and back and swinging side to side

 10/10/10/10

# Knee lift

- Lift your knees alternately forwards and to the side, stretching your arms out
- Make only short ground contact with the ball of the foot

⟳ 10/10

## Sidesteps

- Upper body and arms straight
- Transfer your weight slowly from the right to the left side

↻ 10/10

---

## Side bend

- Cross one leg over the other
- Stretch your arms out over your head
- Bend slowly to the right side and then to the left

↻ 10/10

---

## Punches

- Stand with your feet shoulder width apart
- One hand is holding the club near the club head, the other hand is resting on one knee
- Swing the club head through under the arm

↻ 10/10

## Shoulder rotation

- Stand with your feet shoulder width apart
- Hold your elbows close to your body
- Only rotate your upper body (torso)
- Head, hips and legs stay still

 10/10

---

## lower arm & hand grip

- Stretch out your arms
- Let your fingers move up and down along the grip
- Quickly open and close hand as club drops down warming up lower arm and hand grip muscles

 10/10

---

## Full Body Rotation
## Torso & hips

- Stand with your feet shoulder width apart
- Hold the club with both hands
- Perform a full body rotation mimicking a complete swing

 10/10

*Hit a variety of shots on the range.*

## THE DRIVING RANGE

It's not only for hitting your driver. Try not to rush through your warm-up on the practice range or it may take you several holes to get your game going. Take at least 25-30 minutes warming up and hitting a variety of shots.

After a good dynamic warm-up spend the first 10-15 minutes working on your short game and feel. Avoid only hitting from ideal conditions. Instead try a few more difficult shots, the ones your most likely to encounter on course. As well, mix it up between chips, pitches and sand bunker shots.

Next work on your full swing hitting some balls with more power and purpose. Try to vary as many things as you can from ball to ball to keep the practice random and you thinking about your swing. Vary the club selection, the shape of your shot and the targets you hit to just like you will be forced to do on the course. Never hit the same shot twice in a row, instead if you don't

execute it properly move on and try it again later. Hit some shots mirroring the first hole on the range. First take out your driver and go through your pre-shot routine and set-up hitting the kind of shot you'll want off the first tee. Next go back to your bag for the club you will probably use on your second shot and repeat the routine hitting a long iron or fairway wood, then hit an approach shot with a short iron or wedge to complete the process. Repeat this 2-3 times to help physically, technically and mentally prepare for the first hole. If no access to a range try swinging either a weighted club, club with a weight cuff or 2 clubs at once to get the feel of the rotation needed. Then swinging and brushing the ground or hitting tee's or whiffle balls in the same sequence as above will help prepare you for that first hole. Finish your pre-round practice with some putting on the practice green near the first tee. Practice putting with purpose using only one ball and trying to hole it with each successive putt. Once the ball is in the cup head to a different spot on the green with a different length putt or different slope and configuration and repeat.

Fig. 4.7 / Fig. 4.8 / Fig. 4.9 / Fig. 4.10

Fig. 4.11 / Fig. 4.12

Fig. 4.13 / Fig. 4.14 / Fig. 4.15

## 8-12 MINUTE WARM-UP

Warm-up the hips and challenge balance while switching on your core muscles with leg swings. Start with 2 sets of 10 repetitions of leg swings front and back. Next do 2 sets of 10 leg swings side to side. *See Fig. 4.7 / 4.8 / 4.9 / 4.10*

Now do some torso twists to warm up the upper body and work on rotation and separation. Do 2 sets of 10 repetitions with a club placed on your hips and 2 sets of 10 repetitions with a club placed on your shoulders. *See Fig. 4.11 / 4.12 / 4.13 / 4.14* Next open up the hips with 2 sets of 10 backwards bends. Start slow and go easy so you don't jam your lower back. *See Fig. 4.15*

Fig. 4.16     Fig. 4.17     Fig. 4.18     Fig. 4.19

Fig. 4.20     Fig. 4.21

Fig. 4.22     Fig. 4.23

Next do 2 sets of 10 repetitions of split squat and arm raise combination connecting the upper and lower core. Now move on in the warm-up and open the hips even more by doing some torso turns with club held overhead. Do sets of 10 repetitions. *See Fig. 4.16 / 4.17 / 4.18 / 4.19*

Finish with 2 sets of 10 practice swings starting ½ to ½ swing and progressing to ½ to ¾ and full swing and finally doing a full swing. *See Fig. 4.20 / 4.21 / 4.22 / 4.23*

# Chapter 5

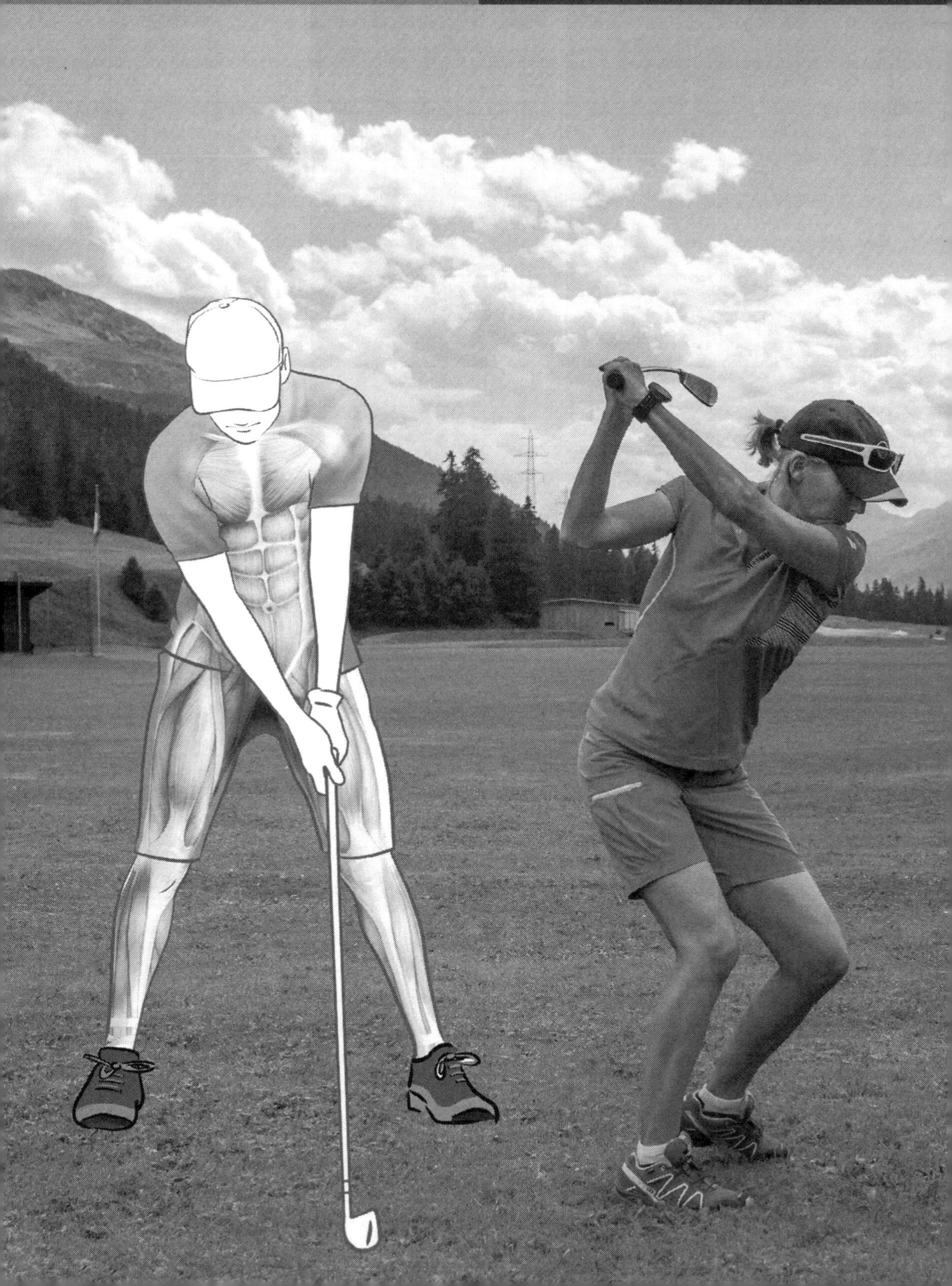

**Strong & Stable Platform = Better Swing**

Golfer's need a strong and stable platform connecting the lower and upper body for a better more consistent swing.

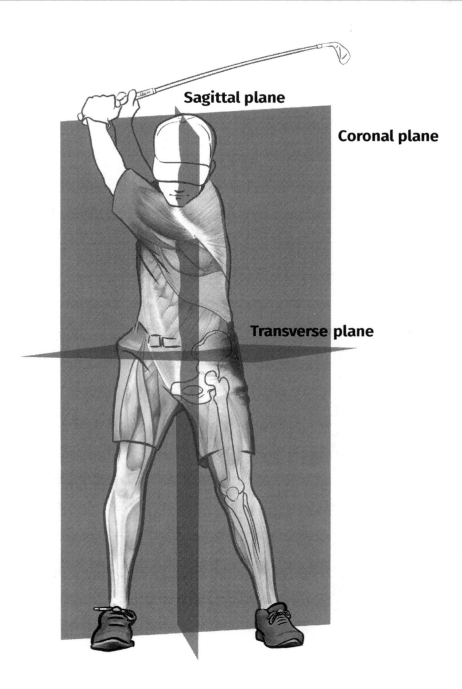

Fig. 5.1

*The body moves through three planes of motion, rotationally (transverse plane), front to back (coronal plane) and side to side (sagittal plane). Much of the swing takes place in the transverse plane. Unfortunately machine based strength and power training lack the ability to easily and adequately strengthen this plane of motion. Effective ball strikers need to be able to dissociate or separate their upper and lower bodies as they make a full swing.*

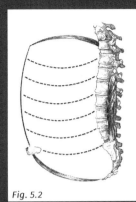

Fig. 5.2

Schematic illustration of inner core cylinder (adapted from Lee, 1999)

Fig. 5.3

Schematic illustration of transverses abdominus (adapted after Celebrini, 2001)

Fig. 5.4

A stable platform of the trunk and hips is needed as you rotate and shift weight during the swing.

# Strong & Stable Platform = Better Swing

You need a strong, stable platform with multi-core stability to create a better swing and protect your back. Even the most technically perfect swing can cause stress to the entire spine including the neck, thoracic and lumbar regions. The muscles of the core (trunk) act as a strong stable platform for the upper and lower extremities to work from and help transfer energy as you rotate and shift weight from the legs through the core (trunk) to the upper body and arms. This is especially important in rotational sports like golf. The golf swing occurs in multiple planes of motion and is a complex blend of muscles and joints working in three dimensions to shorten, lengthen, stabilize, and provide optimum function. *See Fig. 5.1*

The core (trunk) muscles form the stable support base for the body. The inner core consists of four main muscles: 'the inner unit' (Richardson et al., 1999) – the transversus abdominus (TA) (lower abdominals), multifidus (deep, small muscle of the back), the pelvic floor muscles and the diaphragm. Collectively these muscles work together to form a corset-like cylinder of support for the back and pelvis (Lee, 1999). These muscles work together to support the back and pelvis. You want to learn to 'switch on your core' at a low level-like turning up the dimmer switch on a light. *See Fig. 5.2*

Depending on the country, county, gym, or health and fitness professionals and coaches you talk to, they will have different ideas about 'core stability' how to train it, and how to cue it. For the purposes of this book, I will use the cue 'switch on your core' (Petersen & Sirdevan, 2006) Thinking of 'switching on your core' will help connect the upper and lower core musculature through the central core 'inner unit'. You switch your core on at a low level – like turning up the dimmer switch on a light.

## IMPORTANCE OF TRANSVERSUS ABDOMINUS

The transversus abdominus (TA) is the innermost abdominal muscle that connects to the spine at the back and wraps around the trunk to meet its counterpart in the front. It has a large attachment to the lower six ribs and the top of the entire pelvis. When the transversus abdominus contracts, it causes a slight narrowing of the waist and drawing in of the lower abdomen. It functions to stiffen the spine and stabilize the pelvis prior to movements of the arms and legs. In Individuals who use proper stabilization strategies, the transversus abdominus is frequently active at a low level throughout the day. *See Fig. 5.3*

Get a strong and stable upper and lower core by training the inner core and the slings of muscles that run diagonally from the hips to the shoulders with bridging exercises in quadruped, prone, supine, lateral and seated bridge positions. The following exercises are designed to help to develop the core and to strengthen specific larger muscles in a dynamic and functional way. They have been chosen because they are functional in nature and reflect the current research on how our muscles and fascial tissue link together to form sling systems connecting the upper and lower core. The exercises are practical, versatile and can be done anywhere with minimal equipment and useful for golfers of all ages.

**Choose one of the workouts below depending on what you want to work on today:**
- Always do a good dynamic warm up first (see chapter 3 "Dynamic Warm-Up and Cool-Down Guidlines")
- Start slow and progress gradually
- When doing any bridging exercises try to keep spine neutral
- Focus on proper technique (ask a knowledgeable fitness or health professional if you are unsure)
- Perform exercises in a controlled manner
- Choose 2-3 exercises from each program for each session and change them regularly
- Start doing 1-2 sets of 5-10 repetitions and as strength and stability improves increase to 2-3 sets of 10-15 repetitions.

# Switching on Your Core

**Before each exercise think of the following things to effectively switch on your core:**
- Contract the pelvic floor muscles.
- Contract the transversus abdominus (lower abdominals) at a low level.
- The contraction should begin slowly with control (like turning on a dimmer switch) low effort to produce light tension is all that is required

- Remember to breathe normally.
- If standing keep knees soft (slightly bent)

VARIETY IS ONE KEY TO SUCCESS IN FOLLOWING A SMART GOLF TRAINING PROGRAM. IF YOU BECOME BORED, TRY CHANGING THE EXERCISES EACH FEW WEEKS.

# Precautions

## EXERCISE/SWISS BALL PRECAUTIONS

- For individuals new to exercise, check with your physician before starting this or any other exercise program.
- Check your ball for flaws before each use.
- Avoid placing ball near heat or in direct sunlight.
- Avoid sharp objects and jewelry.
- Start gradually and get a feel for the ball before progressing.

## RESISTANCE BAND PRECAUTIONS

- When using resistance tubing or bands, ensure they are of high quality.
- Avoid placing resistance bands near heat or in direct sunlight.
- Avoid sharp objects and jewelry.
- Start gradually and get a feel for the resistance of the bands before progressing or increasing the tension.
- Regularly inspect the stretch band or tubing for wear and tear or weak spots and replace as appropriate.
- Ensure that the band is securely attached or held by a partner you trust before applying resistance.

# Note

**Approach lateral (side) bridging exercises with caution.** If you have shoulder or elbow problems avoid them and see your healthcare professional.

When doing **quadruped bridge exercises** start with hands in line with shoulders and elbows soft (slightly bent) and knees in line with hips. If you have wrist problems try making a fist, placing hands on rolled towels or holding a small dumbbell weight. If the pain persists see your healthcare professional.

# Basework & Bridging A

## Base Work Supine / Lying on your back
## Tighten & Leg Slide

↻ 5-10
⊞ 1-2
🕐 5-0-5

*Start*

*Finish*

- Start lying on your back with both knees bent up
- Switch on your core muscles
- Slowly slide one heel out until leg straight & then back up again to the start position

## Base Work Supine / Lying on your back
## Tighten & Leg Fall Out

⟳ 5-10
⦿ 1-2
⏱ 5-0-5

*Start*

*Finish*

- Start lying on your back with knees bent up
- Switch on your core muscles
- Slowly let one leg fall out to the side & then back up again
  to start position

---

## Base Work Supine / Lying on your back
## Tighten & Scapular Retractions

⟳ 5-10
⦿ 1-2
⏱ 1-1-1

*Start*

*Middle*

*Finish*

- Start lying on your back with knees bent up
- Switch on your core muscles
- Pull a stretch cord apart in 3 different positions

# Clamshell Hip Abduction

↻ 5-10-15
▥ 1-2
⏱ 2-2-1

*Start*

*Finish*

- Start lying on your side with both knees bent up
- Switch on your core & raise one knee up keeping ankles together – like a clam opening its shell
- Hold for 2 seconds & slowly return to start position for a 2 second count
- This exercise can be made more challenging by adding resistance of a resistance band or weight

---

# Side Lying Hip Adduction

↻ 5-10-15
▥ 1-2
⏱ 1-2-1

*Start*

*Finish*

*Variation*

- Start lying on your side with top knee bent & placed floor a ball or small stool
- Keep bottom knee straight
- Switch on your core & raise bottom leg up off the mat
- Hold for 2 seconds & slowly return to start position for a 2 second count
- This exercise can be made more challenging by adding a weight to ankle/foot

## Supine Bridging / lying on your back

⟳ 5-10
▥ 1-2
🕐 1-4-1

*Start*

*Finish*

*Variation*

• Start lying on your back with both knees bent up
• Switch on your core & raise hips off the mat
• Hold for 4 seconds & lower back down to start position
• Do with feet & knees hip width & feet & knees together
• This exercise can be made more challenging by placing a stretch/resistance band
  under back, holding it with one hand and raising arm up

---

## Quadruped Bridge / kneeling on all fours

⟳ 5-10
▥ 1-2
🕐 1-4-1

*Start*

*Middle*

*Finish*

• Start kneeling on all fours with low back arched downward
  like a cow
• Pull/suck belly button up towards spine
• Now arch back up like an angry cat or a camel
• Next, find your neutral position with back flat & hold
  for 4 seconds

# Quadruped Bridge & Single Arm raises

5-10
1-2
1-2-1

*Start*

*Finish right arm*

*Finish left arm*

- Start kneeling on all fours & find your neutral position with back flat
- Switch on your core muscles
- Now raise one arm up & hold for 2 seconds
- Repeat with both arms
- This exercise can be made more challenging by adding weighted resistance to hand

---

# Quadruped Bridge & Single Leg raises

5-10
1-2
1-2-1

*Start*

*Finish right leg*

*Finish left leg*

- Start kneeling on all fours & find your neutral position with back flat
- Switch on your core muscles
- Now raise one leg up & hold
- Repeat with both legs
- This exercise can be made more challenging by adding weighted resistance to the ankle/foot

# Prone Bridging & Hip Twist

↻ 5-10
◫ 1-2
⏱ 1-3-1

Start

Hip twist left

Hip twist right

- Start in a prone bridge position on forearms & toes
- Switch on your core muscles
- Now twist or rotate one side of your hips up & hold

# Lateral Bridging

↻ 5-10
◫ 1-2
⏱ 1-2-1

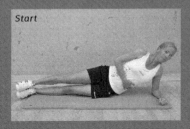
Start

Finish

Variation

- Lying on your side switch on your core
- Start bridging up off knees & progress to bridging off feet
- This exercise can be made more challenging by raising upper arm

(Use with caution if elbow or shoulder problems)

# Basework & Bridging B

## Base Work Supine / Lying on your back
## Tighten & Leg March

↻ 5-10

▥ 1-2

⏱ 10 sec. march

*Start*

*March right leg*

*March left leg*

- Start lying on your back with knees bent up
- Switch on your core muscles
- Slowly march feet up & down

# Base Work Supine / lying on your back Tighten & Arm Leg March

⟳ 5-10
▥ 1-2
🕑 10 sec. march

Start

March right arm/left leg

March left arm/right leg

- Start lying on your back with knees bent up & arms raised up
- Switch on your core muscles
- Slowly move right arm & left leg towards each other
- Repeat with left arm & right leg
- Try doing same side right arm & right leg / left arm & left leg

---

# Side Lying Hip Abduction

⟳ 5-10-15
▥ 1-2
🕑 1-2-1

Start

Finish

- Start lying on your side with bottom knee bent & top knee straight
- Switch on your core
- Point toes down to floor on top leg & raise leg up
- Hold for 2 seconds & down slow for a 2 second count
- This exercise can be made more challenging by adding a weight to ankle/foot

# Supine Bridging & Ball Squeeze

🔄 5-10
⦀ 1-2
🕐 1-4-1

Start

Finish

Variation

- Start lying on your back with both knees bent up & a ball between knees
- Switch on your core & raise hips off the mat lightly squeezing the ball
- Hold for 4 seconds & lower back down to start position
- This exercise can also be done putting a stretch band around knees and pulling apart
- This exercise can be made more challenging by raising one leg up and extending the knee

---

# Supine Bridging & Shoulder Scapular Retractions

🔄 5-10
⦀ 1-2
🕐 1-4-1

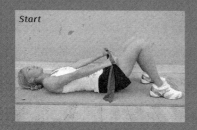
Start

Middle

Finish

- Start lying on your back with both knees bent up & stretch band in both hands
- Switch on your core & raise hips off the mat & pull stretch/resistance band apart in a horizontal and diagonal pattern working the shoulder retractors
- Hold for 4 seconds & lower back down to start position

# Quadruped Bridge with Rocking Movements

⟳ 5-10
▦ 1-2
⊕ 1-0-1 slow

Start

Middle

Finish

- Start kneeling on all fours & find your neutral position with back flat
- Switch on your core muscles
- Now rock into different directions: Forward & back, Side to side, Diagonals, Circles or Figure of 8's

# Quadruped Bridge & Torso Rotation

⟳ 5-10
▦ 1-2
⊕ 1-2-1

Start

Right rotation

Left rotation

- Start kneeling on all fours & find your neutral position with back flat
- Switch on your core muscles
- Now take one arm & thread through other arm rotating torso
- Now rotate torso up raising arm up with elbow bent retracting shoulder
- Repeat with opposite arm

# Prone Bridging on Forearms & Knees

⟳ 5-10
▥ 1-2
🕐 1-5-1 to 1-10-1 to 1-20-1

Start

Finish

Variation

- Start lying in prone/on stomach
- Now bridge up onto knees & forearms
- Switch on your core muscles & find your neutral position with back flat
- Hold for 5-10-20 seconds
- This exercise can be made more challenging by raising up into a full push up position

---

# Prone Bridging & Single Arm Raise

⟳ 5-10
▥ 1-2
🕐 1-3-1 to 1-5-1 to 1-10-1

Start

Finish

Variation

- Start in a prone bridge position on forearms & toes
- Switch on your core muscles
- Now raise up one arm & hold
- This exercise can be made easier by keeping arm bent at the elbow

# Prone Bridging & Single Leg Raise

⟳ 5-10
▥ 1-2
⊕ 1-3-1 to 1-5-1 to 1-10-1

Start

Finish

- Start in a prone bridge position on forearms & toes
- Switch on your core muscles
- Now raise up one leg & hold
- This exercise can be made more challenging by adding weighted resistance to the ankle/foot

# Lateral Bridging with Hip Raise

⟳ 5-10
▥ 1-2
⊕ 1-2-1

Start

Finish

Variation

- Lying on your side switch on your core
- Start bridging up off knees & progress to bridging off feet & raise hip
- This exercise can be made more challenging by raising up one arm & leg or both at the same time

(Use with caution if elbow or shoulder problems)

# Basework & Bridging C

## Base Work Supine / lying on your back
## Tighten & Scapular Retractions

⟳ 5-10

⚙ 1-2

⏱ 1-1-1

*Start*

*Middle*

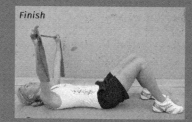

*Finish*

- Start lying on your back with knees bent up
- Switch on your core muscles
- Pull a stretch cord apart in 3 different positions

## Supine Bridging & Double Arm Diagonal Pull

⟳ 5-10
▥ 1-2
🕐 1-4-1

*Start*

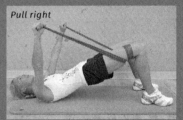
*Pull right*

*Pull left*

- Start lying on your back with both knees bent up & long stretch band around knees
- Switch on your core & raise hips off the mat & diagonally pull stretch band overhead with both arms
- Hold for 4 seconds & lower back down to start position

---

## Quadruped Bridge & Knee Circles

⟳ 5-10
▥ 1-2
🕐 slow

*Start*

*Middle*

*Finish*

- Start kneeling on all fours & find your neutral position with back flat
- Switch on your core muscles
- Now raise one leg off the ground & do slow circles with your knee

## Quadruped Bridge
## Opposite Arm & Leg raises

⟳ 5-10
▥ 1-2
⏱ 1-2-1

Start

Finish right arm/left leg

Finish left arm/right leg

- Start kneeling on all fours & find your neutral position with back flat
- Switch on your core muscles
- Now raise one arm & opposite leg up & hold for 2 seconds
- Repeat with opposite arm & leg

## Quadruped Bridge & Torso Rotations
## with Band Resistance

⟳ 5-10
▥ 1-2
⏱ 1-2-1

Start

Finish

- Start kneeling on all fours & find your neutral position with back flat
- Hold a stretch band in both hands
- Switch on your core muscles
- Now take one arm & thread through other arm rotating torso
- Now rotate torso up raising arm with elbow bent retracting shoulder using stretch band for resistance
- Repeat with opposite arm

# Prone Bridging on Forearms & Toes

⟳ 5-10
⫴ 1-2
⏱ 1-5-1 to 1-10-1 to 1-20-1

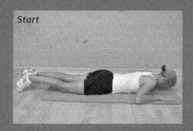
Start

Middle

Finish neutral position

- Start lying in prone/on stomach
- Now bridge up onto toes & forearms
- Switch on your core muscles & find your neutral position with back flat
- Hold for 5-10-20 seconds

# Prone Bridging with Single Arm & Leg Raise

⟳ 5-10
⫴ 1-2
⏱ 1-3-1 to 1-5-1 to 1-10-1

Start

Finish

- Start in a prone bridge position on forearms & toes
- Switch on your core muscles
- Now raise up one leg & one arm up & hold
- Repeat opposite arm and leg

## Prone Bridging
## with Torso Rotation & Arm Raise

↻ 5-10
⦀ 1-2
⏲ 1-3-1

Start

Middle

Finish

- Start in a prone bridge position on forearms & toes
- Switch on your core muscles
- Now twist or rotate your torso & raise one arm up & hold

(Use with caution if elbow or shoulder problems)

## Lateral Bridging
## with Knee Drive & Arm Raise

↻ 5-10
⦀ 1-2
⏲ 1-5-1 to 1-10-1

Start

Middle

Finish

- Lying on your side with forearm on mat
- Switch on your core muscles
- Bridge your hips up then drive knee up to hip height & hold
- Try arm raise & knee drive

(Use with caution if elbow or shoulder problems)

# Lateral Bridging with Arm & Leg Raise

↻ 5-10
▥ 1-2
⏱ 1-5-1 to 1-10-1

Start

Middle

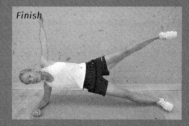
Finish

- Lying on your side with forearm on mat
- Switch on your core muscles
- Bridge your hips up & then raise one arm & one leg up & hold

(Use with caution if elbow or shoulder problems)

Rhomboid Major

Trapezius

Anterior Deltoid

Triceps Brachii

Infraspinatus

Pectoralis Major + Minor

Latissimus Dorsi

Tensor Fasciae Latae

Transversus Abdominis

Gluteus Medius

Gluteus Maximus

Quadriceps

*Base work and bridging exercises improve the stability of the key muscles of a golf swing.*

# Ball, Bands & Balance Bridging A

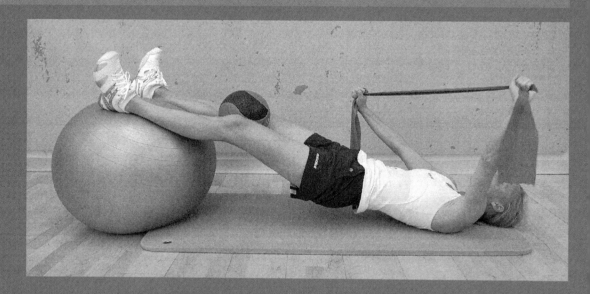

## Quadruped Bridging with Wobble Board

🔄 5-10
📶 1-2
⏱ 1-5-1 to 1-10-1 to 1-20-1

*Start*

*Middle*

*Finish*

- Start kneeling on all fours with hands on a wobble board/ unstable base
- Place knees on the floor or on top of balance rocks/ unstable base
- Find your neutral position with back flat
- Switch on your core muscles
- Now rock back & forth over wobble board for 5 to 20 seconds

# Prone Bridging on Knees or Toes
## Forearms on BOSU® ball

⟳ 5-10
Ⅲ 1-2
⏱ 1-3-1 to 1-5-1 to 1-10-1

*Start*

*Finish*

*Variation*

- Start in a prone bridge position on knees with forearms on a BOSU® ball or other unstable base
- Switch on your core muscles
- Now raise knees up bridging onto toes & hold
- This exercise can be made more challenging by bending one knee and raising it up

---

# Prone Bridging & Knees Up
## Forearms on BOSU® ball

⟳ 5-10
Ⅲ 1-2
⏱ 1-3-1 to 1-5-1 to 1-10-1

*Start*

*Finish*

*Variation*

- Start in a prone bridge position on toes with forearms on a BOSU® ball or other unstable base
- Switch on your core muscles
- Now raise one knee up towards arms & hold
- This exercise can be made more challenging by moving bent leg forward & backward

## Supine Bridging & Ball Squeeze
## Feet on Unstable Base

↻ 5-10
⫿⫿⫿ 1-2
🕐 1-4-1

Start

Finish

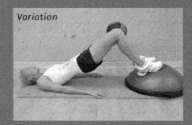
Variation

- Start in a supine bridge position with a ball between your knees & squeeze gently
- Place feet on an unstable base like balance rocks or BOSU® ball
- Switch on your core muscles
- Now raise hips up & hold

## Lateral Bridging
## on Unstable Base

↻ 5-10
⫿⫿⫿ 1-2
🕐 1-2-1

Start

Finish

Variation

- Start lying on your side with forearm on a BOSU® ball or other unstable base
- Switch on your core muscles
- Bridge hips up laterally to spine neutral & hold
- This exercise can be made more challenging by raising upper arm

(Use with caution if elbow or shoulder problems)

# Lateral Bridging on Unstable Base with Leg Raise

↻ 5-10
⦀ 1-2
⏱ 1-5-1 to 1-10-1

Start

Finish

Variation

- Start lying on your side with forearm on a BOSU® ball or other unstable base
- Switch on your core muscles
- Bridge hips up laterally to spine neutral & hold raising upper leg up
- A variation of this exercise would be doing a knee drive

(Use with caution if elbow or shoulder problems)

---

# Supine Bridge & Shoulder Retractions 3 Positions

↻ 5-10-15
⦀ 1-2
⏱ 1-1-1

Start

Middle

Finish

- Start lying on your back with lower leg & feet on a physio ball
- Hold a stretch band in both hands
- Switch on your core muscles
- Bridge hips up & pull stretch band apart retracting shoulder blades in 3 different positions

# Supine Bridge
# with Ball Squeeze & Diagonal Pulls

↻ 5-10-15
⫶ 1-2
🕐 1-1-1

*Start*

*Middle*

*Finish*

- Start lying on your back with lower leg & feet on a physio ball
- Place a small ball between knees & squeeze lightly
- Hold a stretch band in both hands
- Switch on your core muscles
- Bridge hips up & pull stretch band apart in diagonal directions

---

# Sit Downs / Eccentric Abdominals

↻ 8-10-12
⫶ 1-2
🕐 3-0-1

*Start*

*Middle*

*Finish*

- Start sitting on a physio ball with knees together & feet apart
- Switch on your core muscles
- Lean back slowly working your abdominals as they lengthen & return to start position

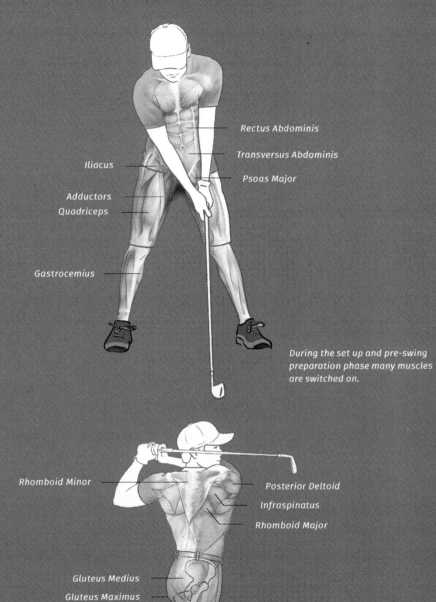

Rectus Abdominis

Transversus Abdominis

Iliacus

Psoas Major

Adductors
Quadriceps

Gastrocemius

During the set up and pre-swing
preparation phase many muscles
are switched on.

Rhomboid Minor

Posterior Deltoid

Infraspinatus

Rhomboid Major

Gluteus Medius
Gluteus Maximus
Hamstrings

Adductors

Gastrocnemius
Soleus

Throughout the swing muscles
are sequentially and rhythmically
activated from the ground up to
create power.

# Ball, Bands & Balance Bridging B

## Quadruped Bridging & Push-Ups on Unstable Base

↻ 5-10
⦀ 1-2
⏱ 1-2-1

*Start*

*Middle*

*Finish*

- Start kneeling on all fours with hands on a wobble board/ unstable base
- Place knees on the floor or on top of balance rocks/unstable base
- Find your neutral position with back flat
- Switch on your core muscles
- Now do a push up over wobble board/unstable base

## Supine Bridging
## Feet on Unstable Base

↻ 5-10
⦀ 1-2
⏱ 1-4-1

Start

Finish

Variation

- Start in a supine bridge position with feet on a BOSU® ball or other unstable base
- Switch on your core muscles
- Now raise hips up & hold

## Lateral Bridging
## on Unstable Base with Knee Drive

↻ 5-10
⦀ 1-2
⏱ 1-5-1 to 1-10-1

Start

Finish

Variation

- Start lying on your side with forearm on a BOSU® ball
- Switch on your core muscles
- Bridge hips up laterally off feet & hold driving upper knee up to hip
- This exercise can be made more challenging by raising upper arm

(Use with caution if elbow or shoulder problems)

# Kneeling Resisted Hip Internal Rotation

⟳ 5-10
▥ 1-2
🕓 1-2-1

Start

Finish

- Start in a kneeling lunge position with one knee on a BOSU® ball or other soft support with hands on wall
- Place a stretch band around ankle & anchored to something stable
- Switch on your core muscles
- Now rotate hip internally against stretch band resistance & back to start position

---

# Kneeling Resisted Hip External Rotation

⟳ 5-10
▥ 1-2
🕓 1-2-1

Start

Finish

- Start in a kneeling lunge position with one knee on a BOSU® ball or other soft support with hands on wall
- Place a stretch band around ankle & anchored to something stable
- Switch on your core muscles
- Now rotate hip externally against stretch band resistance & back to start position

## Seated Horizontal Torso Twists

◯ 8-10-12
⦀ 1-2
⏱ 1-1-1

Start

Finish

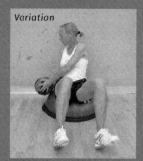
Variation

- Start sitting on the floor, a BOSU® ball or other unstable base
- Hold a medicine ball in hands with arms straight
- Switch on your core muscles
- Now rotate torso & keeping arms horizontal to floor & return back to start position
- A variation of this exercise that is more challenging is lowering the ball to the floor and back up on each side

## Lateral Bridging with Resisted Arm Raise

◯ 5-10
⦀ 1-2
⏱ 2-1-1

Start

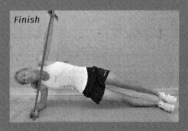
Finish

Variation

- Lying on your side with forearm on mat & holding a stretch band in hands
- Switch on your core muscles
- Bridge your hips up & raise upper arm up against stretch band resistance
- A variation of this exercise is keeping elbow at side and externally rotating the shoulder

(Use with caution if elbow or shoulder problems)

## Supine Bridge & Upper Torso Twist Holding a Ball

↻ 5-10-15
⦀ 1-2
🕐 1-2-1

Start

Rotate right

Rotate left

- Start lying on your back with lower leg & feet on a physio ball
- Switch on your core muscles
- Hold a medicine ball or light weight overhead with arms straight
- Bridge hips up & rotate torso slowly from one side to the other

---

## Supine Bridge & Hamstring Pull Ball between Knees

↻ 5-10
⦀ 1-2
🕐 1-2-1

Start

Middle

Finish

- Start lying on your back with lower leg & feet on a physio ball
- Place a ball between knees & squeeze lightly
- Switch on your core muscles
- Bridge up hips & pull ball towards buttocks & hold for 2 seconds & return to start position

# Prone Bridge
# Feet on Ball & Knee Tuck

↻ 5-10
▥ 1-2
⏱ 1-4-1

- Start in a prone push up position with lower legs on a physio ball & extended out behind you
- Switch on your core muscles
- Pull ball up towards hips maintaining a stable core & keeping a neutral spine position

# Lateral Bridging
# on Physio Ball & Leg Lift

↻ 5-10
▥ 1-2
⏱ 1-5-1 to 1-10-1

- Start in a lateral bridge position with feet on floor and forearm & hand on a physio ball
- Switch on your core muscles
- Place upper hand on hips & raise upper leg into hip abduction & hold
- An easier variation is bridging off knees and upper leg lift

(Use with caution if elbow or shoulder problems)

# Ball, Bands & Balance Bridging C

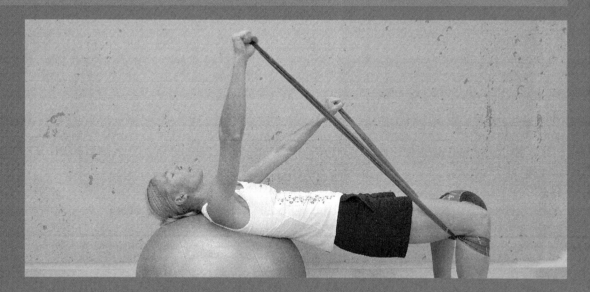

## Quadruped Bridging & Push-Ups on Unstable Base

 5-10
 1-2
 2-1-1

Start

Finish

Variation

- Start kneeling on all fours with hands on a wobble board/ unstable base
- Place knees on the floor or on top of balance rocks/unstable base
- Find your neutral position with back flat
- Switch on your core muscles
- Now do a push up over wobble board/unstable base

# Supine Bridging
# with Balls, Bands & Torso Rotation

⟳ 5-10
▦ 1-2
⏱ 1-1-1

Start

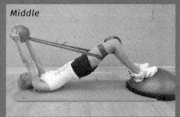
Middle

Finish

- Start in a supine bridge position with feet on a BOSU® ball
- Place a ball in hands & between knees
- Hold a long stretch band anchored to legs
- Switch on your core muscles
- Now squeeze the ball lightly between knees & raise hips up
- Pull arms up & rotate torso with resistance from stretch band

---

# Lateral Bridging
# on Unstable Base with Arm & Leg Raise

⟳ 5-10
▦ 1-2
⏱ 1-5-1 to 1-10-1

Start

Finish

Variation

- Start lying on your side with forearm on a BOSU® ball or other unstable base
- Switch on your core muscles
- Bridge hips up laterally to spine neutral & hold raising both upper arm & leg
- A variation of this exercise is to do an arm raise with upper leg knee drive

(Use with caution if elbow or shoulder problems)

# Seated Hip Internal Rotation & Adduction

5-10
1-2
2-1-1

*Start*

*Middle*

*Finish*

- Start in a seated position on the floor or a BOSU® ball or other unstable base
- Place a stretch band around knee & anchored to something stable
- Switch on your core muscles
- Now adduct & rotate hip internally against stretch band resistance & back to start position

---

# Seated Hip External Rotation & Adduction

5-10
1-2
2-1-1

*Start*

*Finish*

- Start in a seated position on the floor or a BOSU® ball or other unstable base
- Place a stretch band around knee & anchored to something stable
- Switch on your core muscles
- Now abduct & rotate hip externally against stretch band resistance & back to start position

# Seated Diagonal Torso Twists

🔄 8-10-12
⚋ 1-2
🕐 1-1-1

*Start* · *Finish* · *Variation*

- Start sitting on the floor, a BOSU® ball or other unstable base
- Hold a medicine ball in hands with arms straight
- Switch on your core muscles
- Now rotate torso & touch medicine ball close to floor on each side of hips & return back to start position

---

# Supine Bridge
# with Ball Squeeze & Diagonal Pulls

🔄 5-10-15
⚋ 1-2
🕐 1-1-1

*Start* · *Middle* · *Finish*

- Start lying on your back with lower leg & feet on a physio ball
- Place a small ball between knees & squeeze lightly
- Hold a stretch band in both hands
- Switch on your core muscles
- Bridge hips up & pull stretch band apart in diagonal directions

## Supine Bridge & Torso Rotation with Ball Squeeze

5-10-15
1-2
1-2-1

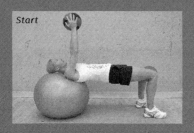
Start

Rotate left

Rotate right

- Start lying with upper back over a physio ball
- Place a small ball between knees & squeeze lightly
- Hold a medicine ball or light weight overhead with arms straight
- Switch on your core muscles
- Rotate torso slowly from one side to the other

## Supine Bridge over Physio Ball & Diagonal Pulls

5-10 / position
1-2
1-5-1 to 1-10-1 to 1-20-1

Start

Pull right

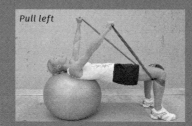
Pull left

- Start lying with upper back over a physio ball
- Place a small ball between knees & squeeze lightly
- Hold a stretch band in hands & anchored to legs
- Switch on your core muscles
- Raise arms up in a diagonal pattern against stretch band resistance

# Supine Bridge
# with Back Extension & Arm Extension

○ 5-10-15
(III) 1-2
🕒 3-0-1

Start

Middle

Finish

- Start lying with upper back over a physio ball
- Place a small ball between knees & squeeze lightly
- Hold a medicine ball in hands against stomach
- Switch on your core muscles
- Raise medicine ball up & overhead working the abdominal muscles as they lengthen

**These exercises are not exhaustive and you may add others based on your experience or on the advice of your health or fitness professional.**

## RULES OF CORE STRENGTH

- Do some form of multi-core (upper & lower) training on a daily basis.
- Always start with 'Switching on Your Core' routine to reeducate the lower abdominals to work in a pre-anticipatory way. This is especially important after a lay off, after an injury, or when you have been mal-aligned or have low back or hip pain and stiffness.
- Approach traditional sit-ups with caution, as the elbow-knee movement places a lot of strain on the low back.
- Core exercises should be done at the end of training or strength work outs so that they can adequately function as stabilizers during the training session before you fatigue them.

Fig. 5.5     Fig. 5.6     Fig. 5.7

*Proper posture and both lower and upper core stability are needed for an effective full swing.*

# Upper Core Stability Proper Posture Helps Technique

The poor postural positions we assume during work, while driving and at school can often lead to muscle imbalances about the shoulder, neck and upper back. Forward head posture and associated scapular dysfunction (winging) is common in many golfers due to our predominantly sedentary/ seated work lifestyle and use of computers and hand held devices. Compounding this problem is that most sports are played with the shoulders rounded forward. In this position the shoulder can be vulnerable to injury with any swinging or overhead motion due to the shoulder sitting in an anterior position. The muscles that internally rotate the shoulder including pectoralis major, anterior deltoid, subscapularis and latissimus dorsi are typically stronger than the external rotators made up of the posterior deltoid and infraspinatus. This is especially pronounced on the dominant side.

Shoulder dysfunction and pain is often caused or worsened by this poor posture and/or an imbalance in strength and length of the muscles around the shoulder and scapula. When swinging the club with a dysfunctional posture your muscles have difficulty shortening, stabilizing and lengthening throughout the swing and the proper mechanics are compromised. Your swing becomes a series of compensations instead of a smooth proper swing with sound joint and muscle mechanics.

# Brief Anatomy Lesson

The shoulder (glenohumeral joint) is a ball and socket joint which is an inherently unstable bony structure. Its stability comes from ligaments and a capsule that surrounds it and provides static control. The dynamic control comes mainly from the muscles of the rotator cuff, as well as those muscles that control the movement of the scapula. The rotator cuff muscles are the supraspinatus, infraspinatus, teres minor and subscapularis. A strong rotator cuff plays an essential role in transferring or funneling the power from the ground up through the torso to the arms.

The muscles that control the movement of the scapula are the serratus anterior, inferior trapezius and rhomboids. Since the scapula needs to move in coordination with the arm, these scapular muscles are as important as the rotator cuff muscles for smooth, efficient movement of the arm. Lack of strength or control of any of these muscles can result in rotator cuff impingement, especially in people who do lots of swinging or overhead activity.

For golfers ground-based free-weight and stretch band resistance exercises with varying levels of balance instability applied at different points should be included as exercises to train connect the core stability. These exercises help promote proper muscle balance by putting emphasis on exercising muscles that are often overlooked and add additional force vectors of resistance to traditional training methods. They also promote stability in regions of musculature that are often weak as a result

of training and playing overuse that results in fatigue, active trigger points and palpable tissue tension.

By utilizing simple equipment including stretch bands to strengthen the upper core and improve stability and posture we can help players develop a stable upper core platform needed to funnel the forces generated in a proper golf swing. Always ensure your chin is tucked in slightly to keep the head in line with the spine and set your shoulder blades to keep your back straight. If you try to swing from a hunched upper back and forward head posture you will tend to rise up during the ball impact creating faults. Other common swing faults that result from poor posture can include hip slide and a flat backswing.

The following exercises are designed to stabilize the shoulder girdle and strengthen the rotator cuff muscles. Perform them after a light warm-up of simple arm circles and swings or after a few minutes on an elliptical trainer or rowing ergometer.

*Shoulder girdle muscles must accelerate and decelerate to funnel the power generated from the lower core and legs to the arms during a full swing.*

Upper Trapezius
Posterior Deltoid
Mid Trapezius
Infraspinatus
Teres Minor
Rhomboid Major
Latissimus Dorsi
Internal Obliques
External Obliques

# Upper Core Stability

---

## Shoulder Rows

5-10-15
1-2
2-0-1

Start

Finish

- Start standing up holding 2 ends of a stretch band
- Switch on your core muscles
- Pull the band back close to your hips sliding shoulder blades together

## Shoulder Retractions Letter I

5-10-15
1-2
2-0-1

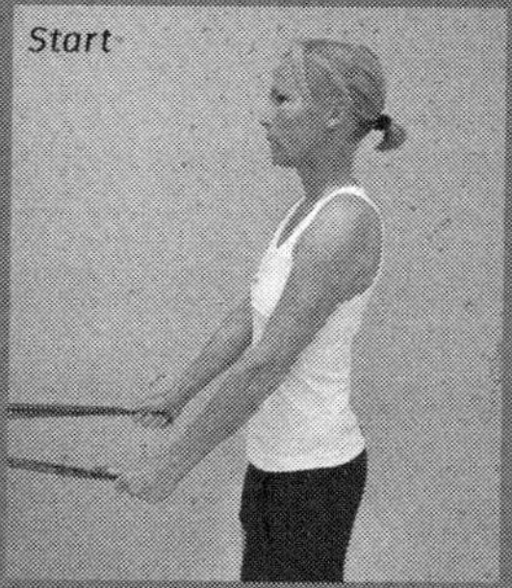
Start

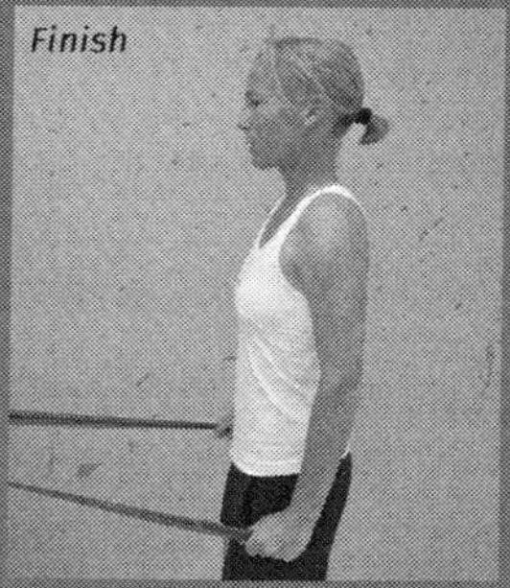
Finish

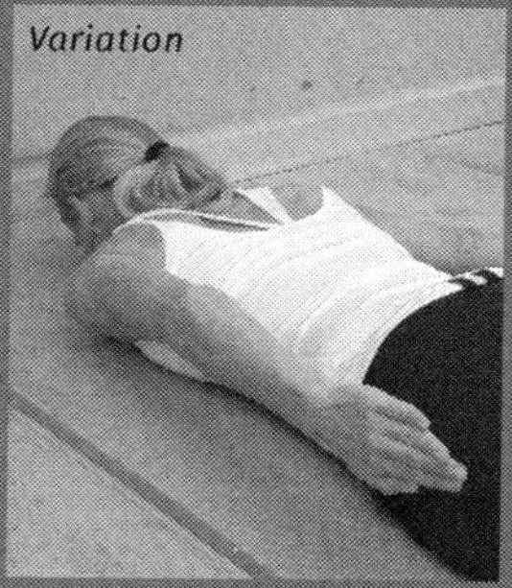
Variation

- Start in standing holding 2 ends of a stretch band
- Switch on your core muscles
- Keep arms straight & pull the band back close to your hips as you slide shoulder blades together
- An easier variation is doing this exercise in a prone position

---

## Shoulder Retractions Letter A

5-10-15
1-2
2-0-1

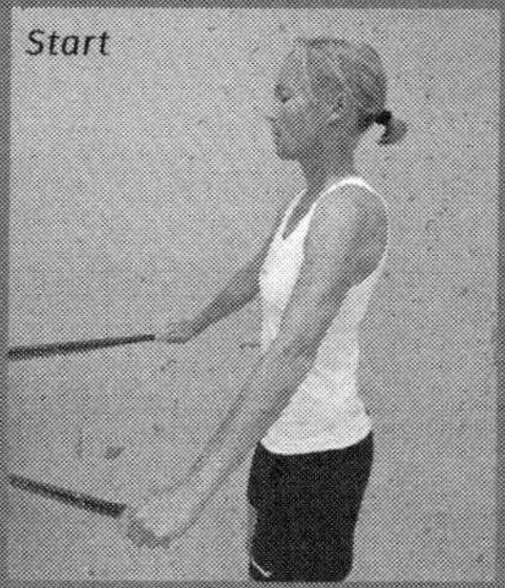
Start

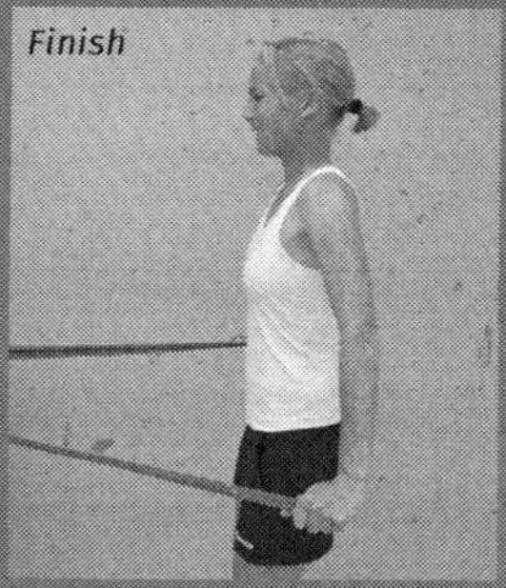
Finish

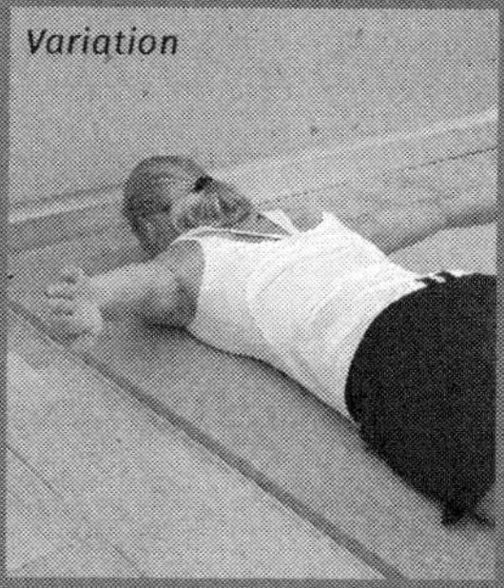
Variation

- Start in standing holding 2 ends of a stretch band
- Switch on your core muscles
- Keep arms at 45 degrees & pull the bands back sliding shoulder blades together
- An easier variation is doing this exercise in a prone position

## Shoulder Retractions
## Letter T

↻ 5-10-15
⦀ 1-2
⏱ 2-0-1

Start

Finish

- Start in standing holding 2 ends of a stretch band
- Switch on your core muscles
- With elbows bent to just 90 degrees & arms up just below shoulder height pull the bands back
- Slide shoulder blades together
- Return to start position

---

## Shoulder Retractions
## Letter W

↻ 5-10-15
⦀ 1-2
⏱ 2-0-1

Start

Finish

Variation

- Start in standing holding 2 ends of a stretch band with arms in front
- Switch on your core muscles
- With elbows bent to 90 degrees & arms at shoulder height pull the bands back
  as you slide shoulder blades together
- An easier variation is doing this exercise in a prone position

# Shoulder External Rotations

⟳ 5-10-15
▥ 1-2
🕑 2-0-1

Start     Finish     Variation

- Start in standing holding a stretch cord in one hand
- Keep elbow at your side with a rolled towel or something similar between elbow & torso
- Switch on your core muscles
- Pull band away from your body
- Return to start position
- If doing this without something between elbow and waist, ensure the elbow stays touching waist

---

# Serratus Punch with Lunge

⟳ 5-10-15
▥ 1-2
🕑 2-0-1

Start     Finish     Variation

- Start in standing holding a stretch band in one hand
- Switch on your core muscles
- Punch arm forward against the stretch band resistance as you lunge forward onto the opposite leg
- Repeat on both sides
- Return to start position
- A variation of this exercises is punching the hand out a higher angle

# Shoulder Diagonal Pulls

⟳ 5-10-15
⦀ 1-2
🕐 2-0-1

*Start*

*Pull on diagonal*

*Pull opposite diagonal*

- Start in standing holding 2 ends of a stretch band
- Switch on your core muscles
- Do a diagonal pull with arms separating hands & repeat in both diagonals

---

# Shoulder Depressions

⟳ 5-10-15
⦀ 1-2
🕐 2-0-1

*Start*

*Finish*

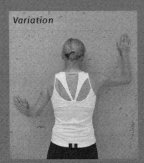
*Variation*

- Start in standing holding 2 ends of a stretch band with shoulder blade raised up
- Switch on your core muscles
- Do a shoulder depression sliding shoulder blade down against stretch band resistance
- Return to start position & repeat on both sides
- Wall push ups in a variety of positions also improve upper core stability

# Scapular Retractions

⟳ 5-10-15

▥ 1-2

🕐 1-2-1

Start

Finish

Variation

- Start in standing holding a stretch band in both hands & firmly anchored to something in front of you
- Pull stretch band to your chest & then pull band apart squeezing shoulder blades together and hold
- Control it as you return slowly to the start position
- A variation of this exercise is doing a single arm retraction in a bent over position with the stretch/resistance band anchored under feet

**By adding in the upper core posture exercises you will promote a more stable upper core platform to swing from. By keeping your back flat with improved posture you can more easily and repeatedly turn your shoulders around your spine axis during the swing producing more consistent contact and ball speed.**

## Chapter 6

**Connecting Your Core for a Stronger Game**

Improve performance, hit the ball further and more consistently with less chance of injury by making connecting your core an important focus of training.

# Connecting Your Core for a Stronger Game

Historically many golfer's avoided traditional strength training methods fearing it would slow down their swing and make them too muscular interfering with the suppleness needed to perform on course. However, the changing nature and demands of the modern game means that golfer's need to be more powerful and stronger than players of generations past. With these increased training demands and participation by ever younger players we must be proactive in our training of these developing athletes as well as with more mature players.

Over the last two decades strength and stability training for golfers has become increasingly common and is included in the yearly periodization plan. Properly planned strength training of the upper core and arms and lower core and legs (hips) will enhance on course performance and allow players to increase maximal force and power to optimize training and as well protect against injury. The goals of the program will be to increase stability in all three planes of motion with functional exercise progressions.

Golf is a controlled methodical sport interspersed with explosive bursts of torque and rotation as you swing the club to strike the ball. The average number of swings on the practice range could be anywhere from 30-300 balls. The number of shots you take while playing depends on your handicap, how many holes you play and how well you stroke the ball. Walking a round of golf may take from 3.5 to 5.5 hours of walking over 6,200 to 7,000 yards on undulating ground. You can probably add another 1,000 yards to that if you're not always hitting the ball straight down the middle. As well golfers bend down to the ground from 36-100 times in a regular round to tee up the ball, inspect it for dirt and retrieve it from the cup.

If you want to hit the ball further, more consistently and be pain free both during and after a golf game following a core strength and stability regimen should be high on your to do list. All players want to hit with power and add distance to their drives. As well they want to have a more accurate short game yet many do not consider it important to do physical conditioning to improve their stroke performance. For a beginning player getting an early start on your golf strength and stability training program will help you create a healthy, aligned, balanced base on which to build the fundamentals of a good consistent swing. It will also help you stay pain and injury free. For players that are more mature and experienced it is never too late to address the potential physical imbalances that have occurred with years of working and playing. Proper golf specific fitness also helps give you a significant competitive advantage and lower your handicap.

Swinging the golf club involves movements that pass through many planes of motion and create rotational and torsional forces on numerous joints and muscles at the same time. The sequence of the swing should be pushing from the ground up, firing your dominant side and leading with the legs and lower core, then transferring and funneling the energy and power through the upper core and arms to the club (*See Fig. 6.1 / 6.2*).

Fig. 6.1          Fig. 6.2

*Significant forces are placed on the kinetic chain from the hips to the ground.*

If a golfer's alignment, balance control, connected core stability, deceleration strength and extended hip stability required to carry out a good swing are not optimal they may be at risk of injury. When designing strength and stability training programs for golfers one must keep these specific directions of movement and additional needs in mind for the different physical components.

## INJURY CONCERNS FOR GOLFERS

Physiotherapists, physicians, coaches and fitness trainers are all well aware of the importance of upper and lower core stability training to a golfers overall development, performance and injury prevention. Functional data suggests that elite adolescents possess poor proprioception, strength and agility in key spine stabilizers, including multifidus, iliopsoas and transversus abdominus (Alyas et al, 2007). We can assume that elite and non-elite golfers may also have the same concerns. If there is inadequate development of the stable platforms of the upper core and arms and lower core and legs the golfer may be unable to perform to their potential and may be at risk of injury.

Lower back pain is a common concern and complaint of golfers. Weaknesses and imbalances of the core have been related to low back pain (Akuthoto & Nadler, 2004) and lower extremity injuries (Ireland et al, 2003). As well a study looked at core stability parameters and found that weakness in hip external rotation was correlated with incidence of knee injury (Leetun et al, 2004). Hip strength and flexibility is also important since decreased hip flexibility in rotation or decreased strength in abduction was often seen in athletes with shoulder problems which is another common golf complaint.

Hip abduction strength and stability is a key to a powerful swing. Prior to impact as much as 2–3 times a golfer's body weight is placed on the hips. Players with weak hips may commit swing errors more often that can limit on course performance and over time can lead to injury.

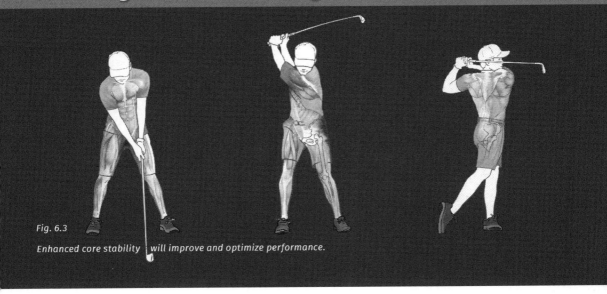

*Fig. 6.3*

*Enhanced core stability will improve and optimize performance.*

Very few recreational or competitive golfers make it through an entire season without experiencing some form of lumbar and torso issues or lower extremity and upper extremity injuries associated with kinetic chain weakness and/or malalignment syndrome. Abnormal or malalignment syndrome and associated biomechanical changes can contribute to injury in players due to imbalances of muscle length and strength. The subsequent increased tissue tension can cause overuse and tissue breakdown. Athletes who suffer from malalignment syndrome may have difficulty progressing in their sport and, as a result sometimes have to abandon their efforts all together (Schamberger, 2002). This malalignment syndrome can be exacerbated by the unilateral (one sided) nature of the golf swing placing abnormal rotational and deceleration stresses on the body. Malalignment syndrome may also put golfers at increased risk of injury and once injured, they are likely to take longer to recover.

## IMPORTANCE OF THE CORE

In golfers, the abdominal musculature plays a significant role in core stability providing a muscular link between the lower and upper extremities. The core musculature includes muscles of the trunk and pelvis that are responsible for the maintenance of stability of the spine and pelvis and help in generation and lateral transfer of weight and energy from the large to small body parts during the swing.

There are four commonly accepted global muscle slings that should be addressed when designing multi-planar exercises that mimic the acceleration, deceleration, diagonal patterns, rotational and stability needs of the golf swing. They attach in groups forming functional slings from the hips through the lumbo-pelvic (lower core) to the scapula-thoracic (upper core) regions. Four slings of muscle systems have been described in the literature (Vleeming et al, 1995) (Snijders et al, 1993). These are the posterior oblique sling, the anterior oblique sling, the

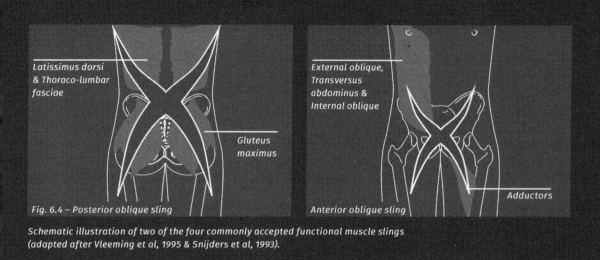

Latissimus dorsi
& Thoraco-lumbar
fasciae

Gluteus
maximus

Fig. 6.4 – Posterior oblique sling

External oblique,
Transversus
abdominus &
Internal oblique

Adductors

Anterior oblique sling

Schematic illustration of two of the four commonly accepted functional muscle slings
(adapted after Vleeming et al, 1995 & Snijders et al, 1993).

longitudinal sling and the lateral sling. These slings of muscles help transfer and funnel the energy from the legs through the core (trunk) to the upper body and arms. This is especially important in swinging sports like golf that involve diagonal patterns of movements with rotation and deceleration. *See Fig. 6.4*

## WHY CONNECT THE UPPER & LOWER CORE?

Upper and lower core strength training provides a stable three-dimensional power platform from which the extremities can work during multi-planar, multi-joint, and multi-muscle activities that involve acceleration and deceleration forces (Petersen, 2005). Utilizing closed and partially closed chain exercises with varied resistance to increase stability of the posterior oblique and anterior oblique sling helps improve the golfer's ability to brace, accelerate, transfer weight laterally and decelerate a swinging motion. Adding additional exercises to promote involvement of the lateral and longitudinal

sling will further help to connect your core and improve stability.

Research has demonstrated that lower extremity position influences scapular muscle recruitment and muscle balance ratios in closed kinetic chain exercises (Maenhout et al, 2009). As well, trunk and lower extremity position and movement influence scapular muscle recruitment and muscle balance ratios in open kinetic chain exercises (De Mey et al, 2012). An explanation of chain exercises can be found in Chapter 2 The ABC's of Smart Golf Training.

The challenge for busy clinicians, golf and fitness coaches is how to effectively prescribe connect your core exercises that ensure optimal recruitment, balance, timing, deceleration control and mimic the performance demands of golf. Individuals are best suited to rotational motion, torque and angular movement with full kinetic chain involvement. But many commonly prescribed fitness room exercises are machine based and involve or isolate a single joint only

# Connecting Your Core for a Stronger Game

Fig. 6.5

Fig. 6.6

Fig. 6.7

Fig. 6.8

*Always warm-up with leg swings front & back and side to side. Do 2 sets of 10 repetitions.*

allowing movement in one or two planes of motion without full kinetic chain involvement. They do not always address the finer aspects of postural awareness during weight transfer through the kinetic chain or ensure your body trains in all three planes of motion. To enhance a powerful swing the upper to lower core must be able to wind up and coil or dissociate.

Connecting your core with multidirectional upper and lower core stability training provides smart training strategies that can be taught to golfers of all ages. The focus of connecting your core exercises should follow the ABC's of smart training A-alignment, B-balance, C-closed and partially closed kinetic chain exercises and D-deceleration strength in a E-extended hip position.

## BENEFITS OF CONNECT YOUR CORE STABILITY TRAINING

- Improves postural set and helps maintain correct pelvic alignment
- Improves strength of functional muscle slings that connect the upper and lower core
- Improves joint and muscle position sense (kinesthetic awareness), helping to center the joint and absorb stress
- Improves stability in a functional hip-extended position
- Improves ability to counter-rotate or dissociate

- the upper and lower torso and extremities
- Improves dynamic balance and movement efficiency
- Adds additional force vectors of resistance to traditional training methods
- Helps to improve athletic performance and helps the body to be able to react to unexpected events
- Provides exercises that are versatile, practical, transportable and affordable

Fig. 6.9    Fig. 6.10    Fig. 6.11    Fig. 6.12

*Do 2 sets of 10–15 repetitions of double leg squats (keeping knees over toes) while retracting scapula.*

*Do 2 sets of 10-15 repetitions doing this rotational swinging motion on unstable surface. Do both high to low and low to high.*

Following are numerous exercises that can be implemented on an ongoing basis to help connect your core, enhance stability and improve your golf swings rhythm, timing, balance, acceleration and ensure solid contact.

## WARM-UP FIRST

Before starting this or any exercise routine do some light dynamic warm-up exercises like leg swings *(See Fig. 6.5–6.8)*, high knees and crossover runs (not shown). Always 'switch on your core' (like turning up the dimmer switch on a light) (Petersen, 2006a) to help connect the core muscles. Using this cue while doing core stability exercises will help connect the upper and lower core musculature through the central core 'inner unit'. This "inner unit" (Richardson et al., 1999) consists of four main muscles: the transversus abdominus (TA, i.e., lower abdominals), multifidus (deep, small muscle of the back), the pelvic floor muscles, and the diaphragm.

Doing some double leg squats with a large physio/stability ball at your back will help lubricate the joins of the lower extremity. As well retracting your scapula at the same time gets the posterior cuff muscles sliding the scapula around the thorax. Add a rotational and balance component to the warm-up by doing low to high torso rotations standing on an unstable base. *See Fig. 6.9–6.12*

For golfers ground-based free-weight and stretch band resistance exercises with varying levels of balance instability applied at different points should be included as exercises to train connect your core stability. These exercises help promote proper muscle balance by putting emphasis on exercising muscles that are often overlooked. The prescribed programs should be individualized to the age, experience and fitness level of the golfer. As a general rule choose a few (6-8) exercises from 1 program or mix and match based on your training needs. Generally start with 1-2 sets of 5-10 repetitions and progress to 2-3 sets of 10-15 repetitions. Use a slow tempo.

# Connect Your Core A

## Supine Bridging & Ball Squeeze with Single Arm Diagonal Pull

5-10

1-2

1-4-1

Start

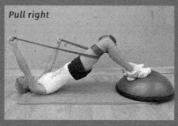

Pull right

Pull left

- Start in a supine bridge position with feet on a BOSU® ball or other unstable base
- Place a ball between your knees & squeeze gently
- Hold a long stretch band anchored to legs
- Switch on your core muscles
- Raise hips up & pull one arm diagonally back with resistance from the stretch band

## Supine Bridge & Medicine Ball Arm Raise with Stretch Band

↻ 5-10-15
▥ 1-2
⏱ 1-4-1

Start

Middle

Finish

- Start lying with upper back over a physio ball
- Place a small ball between knees & squeeze lightly
- Hold a medicine ball in hands along with a stretch band anchored to legs
- Switch on your core muscles
- Raise medicine ball overhead with both arms against stretch band resistance

## Supine Bridging & Single Arm Band Pull with Ball Squeeze

↻ 5-10-15
▥ 1-2
⏱ 1-4-1

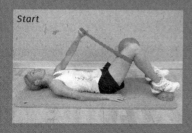
Start

Finish

Variation

- Start lying on your back with both feet on an unstable base like balance rocks or a wobble board.
- Grasp a stretch band in one hand with other end anchored around your leg
- Place a small ball between knees & squeeze lightly
- Switch on your core muscles
- Bridge hips up & move arm in a diagonal pattern against resistance

# Connecting Your Core for a Stronger Game

## Quadruped Bridge & Single Arm Raise with Band Resistance

↺ 5-10
⊟ 1-2
⏱ 1-2-1

Start

Finish

- Start kneeling on all fours with knees on an unstable base like balance rocks
- Place a stretch band around one knee and hold it in one hand
- Find your neutral position with back flat
- Switch on your core muscles
- Now raise one arm up against stretch band resistance & hold for 2 seconds
- Repeat with both arms

---

## Quadruped Bridge & Resisted Torso Rotations on Unstable Base

↺ 5-10
⊟ 1-2
⏱ 2-1-1

Start

Middle

Finish

- Start on all fours & find your neutral position with back flat
- Attach a stretch band to both hands
- Switch on your core muscles
- Now take one arm & thread through other arm rotating torso
- Now rotate torso up raising arm with elbow bent retracting shoulder against resistance of stretch band
- Repeat with opposite arm

# Split Squat on Ball with Resisted Torso Rotation

↻ 5-10-15
⫴ 1-2
⏱ 1-2-1

*Start*

*Middle*

*Finish*

- Start sitting on am physio ball in a split squat position
- Hold a stretch band in your hands with elbows straight
- Switch on your core muscles
- Rotate torso with resistance from stretch band & hold for 2 seconds

---

# Lateral Sit-Ups on Ball

↻ 8-10-12
⫴ 1-2
⏱ 2-0-1

*Start*

*Finish*

- Start lying on your side over a physio ball
- Place feet against a stable surface
- Switch on your core muscles
- Raise your torso up laterally & return slowly to start position
- Repeat on both right and left sides

## Ball Squats &
## Shoulder External Rotation

⟳ 5-10-15
⦙ 1-2
⏱ 2-0-1-to 4-0-1

Start

Finish

- Start standing tall with a physio ball at your back
- Hold a stretch band in both hands with elbows at your side
- Switch on your core muscles
- Squat down keeping knees aligned over toes & externally rotate shoulders against stretch band resistance

---

## Split Squat &
## Shoulder Upright Single or Double Arm Rows

⟳ 5-10-15
⦙ 1-2
⏱ 2-0-1 to 4-0-1

Start

Finish

- Start in a split squat position in front of a physio ball with right lower leg on ball
- Hold a stretch/resistance band in one or both hands with arms straight
- Switch on your core muscles
- Do a split squat down pulling stretch band up into an upright row

# Squat & Shoulder Forward Press

5-10-15
1-2
2-0-1 to 4-0-1

Start

Finish

- Start in a squat position with a physio ball at your back
- Hold a stretch band in both hands firmly anchored to your thigh
- Switch on your core muscles
- Do a squat down pushing stretch band out into a shoulder press

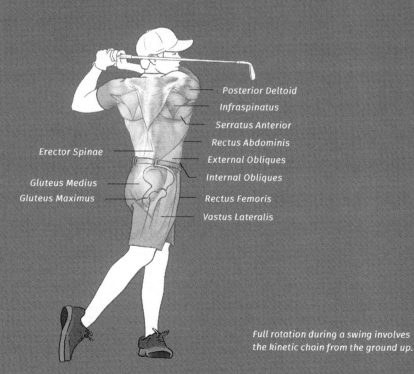

Posterior Deltoid
Infraspinatus
Serratus Anterior
Rectus Abdominis
Erector Spinae
External Obliques
Internal Obliques
Gluteus Medius
Gluteus Maximus
Rectus Femoris
Vastus Lateralis

Full rotation during a swing involves the kinetic chain from the ground up.

# Connect Your Core B

## Supine Bridging & Ball Squeeze with Double Arm Diagonal Pull

↻ 5-10
⫾⫾ 1-2
⏱ 1-4-1

*Start*

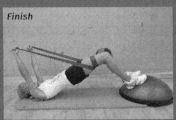
*Finish*

- Start in a supine bridge position with feet on a BOSU® ball or other unstable base
- Place a ball between your knees & squeeze gently
- Hold a long stretch band anchored to legs
- Switch on your core muscles
- Raise hips up & pull both arms diagonally back with resistance from the stretch band

# Supine Bridge over Physio Ball & Knee Extension

○ 5-10
(III) 1-2
⏱ 2-1-1

Start

Right knee extension

Left knee extension

- Start lying with upper back over a physio ball
- Place a small ball between knees & squeeze lightly
- Hold a stretch band in hands & anchored to legs
- Switch on your core muscles
- Raise arms up in a diagonal pattern against stretch band resistance as you extend one knee

---

# Prone Bridge Feet on Ball & Walk Arms Out

○ 5-10 / position
(III) 1-2
⏱ 1-2-1

Start

Finish

- Start in a prone push up position with lower legs on a physio ball
- Switch on your core muscles
- Walk arms out until legs straight & hold for 2 seconds then return to start position

## Supine Bridge & Medicine Ball Torso Rotation with Stretch Band

↻ 5-10-15
▥ 1-2
⏱ 1-2-1

*Start*

*Rotate right*

*Rotate left*

- Start lying with upper back over a physio ball
- Place a small ball between knees & squeeze lightly
- Hold a medicine ball in hands along with a stretch band anchored to legs
- Switch on your core muscles
- Raise medicine ball overhead & rotate torso from side to side slowly

## Split Squat on Ball with Straight Arm Torso Rotation

↻ 5-10-15
▥ 1-2
⏱ 1-1-1

*Start*

*Middle*

*Finish*

- Start sitting on a physio ball in a split squat position
- Hold a medicine ball in hands at waist height
- Switch on your core muscles and straighten arms
- Rotate torso rotating the medicine ball back & forth

# Ball Squats with Ball Squeeze & Shoulder External Rotation

↻ 5-10-15
⦿ 1-2
🕐 2-0-1 to 4-0-1

Start

Finish

- Start standing tall with a physio ball at your back
- Hold a stretch band in both hands with elbows at your side & place a ball between knees
- Switch on your core muscles
- Squat down keeping knees aligned over toes while lightly squeezing ball between knees
- Externally rotate shoulders against stretch band resistance as you squat down

---

# Split Squat & Shoulder Press

↻ 5-10-15
⦿ 1-2
🕐 2-0-1 to 4-0-1

Start

Finish

- Start in a split squat position in front of a physio ball with right lower leg on ball
- Hold a stretch band in right hand with other end firmly anchored
- Switch on your core muscles
- Do a split squat down pushing stretch band up into a shoulder press

## Split Squat &
## Shoulder Forward Press

⟳ 5-10-15
▥ 1-2
⏱ 2-0-1 to 4-0-1

Start

Finish

- Start in a split squat position with a physio ball at your back
- Hold a stretch band in both hands firmly anchored to your thigh
- Switch on your core muscles
- Do a split squat down pushing stretch band out into a shoulder press

---

## Squat, Ball Squeeze &
## Shoulder Forward Press

⟳ 5-10-15
▥ 1-2
⏱ 2-0-1 to 4-0-1

Start

Finish

- Start in a squat position with a physio ball at your back
- Place a ball between knees
- Hold a stretch band in both hands firmly anchored to your thigh
- Switch on your core muscles
- Do a squat down pushing stretch band out into a shoulder press

# Squat, Ball Squeeze & Lateral Raise with Bicep Curl

5-10-15
1-2
2-0-1 to 4-0-1

Start

Finish

- Start in a squat position with a physio ball at your back
- Place a ball between knees
- Hold a stretch band in both hands firmly anchored under your feet
- Switch on your core muscles
- Do a squat down as you lightly squeeze ball between knees
- Do a bicep curl with one arm while raising the other into elevation squat down

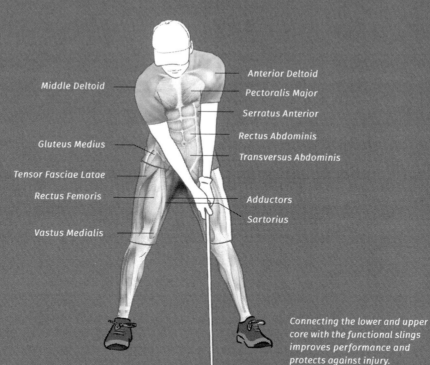

Middle Deltoid

Gluteus Medius

Tensor Fasciae Latae

Rectus Femoris

Vastus Medialis

Anterior Deltoid

Pectoralis Major

Serratus Anterior

Rectus Abdominis

Transversus Abdominis

Adductors

Sartorius

Connecting the lower and upper core with the functional slings improves performance and protects against injury.

# Connect Your Core C

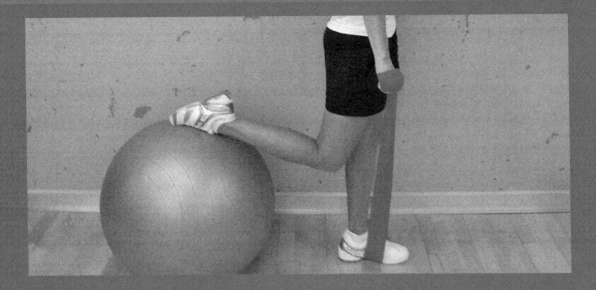

## Supine Bridge & Hamstring Pull
## with Stretch Band Diagonal Pull

↻ 5-10-15
⦀ 1-2
⊕ 1-2-1

*Start*

*Middle*

*Finish*

- Start lying on your back with lower leg & feet on a physio ball
- Switch on your core muscles
- Hold a long stretch band in out-stretched hands & anchored to legs
- Bridge hips up & pull stretch band back in a diagonal direction

## Supine Bridging & Double Arm Band Pull with Ball Squeeze

↻ 5-10-15
⦀ 1-2
⏱ 1-4-1

- Start lying on your back with both feet on an unstable base like balance rocks
- Grasp a stretch band in both hands with other end anchored around your leg
- Place a small ball between knees & squeeze lightly
- Switch on your core muscles
- Bridge hips up & move arms in a diagonal pattern against resistance

---

## Split Squat on Ball with Bent Arm Torso Rotation

↻ 5-10-15
⦀ 1-2
⏱ 1-1-1

- Start sitting on a physio ball in a split squat position
- Hold a medicine ball in hands with elbows bent
- Switch on your core muscles
- Rotate torso rotating the medicine ball back & forth

## Ball Squats with Ball Squeeze & Shoulder Diagonal Pull

↻ 5-10-15
⦀ 1-2
🕐 2-0-1 to 4-0-1

*Start*

*Finish*

- Start standing tall with a physio ball at your back
- Hold a stretch band in both hands with elbows at your side & place a ball between knees
- Switch on your core muscles
- Squat down keeping knees aligned over toes while lightly squeezing ball between knees
- Do a diagonal pull against stretch band resistance as you squat down

---

## Split Squat & Shoulder Diagonal Pull

↻ 5-10-15
⦀ 1-2
🕐 2-0-1 to 4-0-1

*Start*

*Finish*

- Start in a split squat position in front of a physio ball with right lower leg on ball
- Hold a stretch band in right hand with other end firmly anchored
- Switch on your core muscles
- Do a split squat down pulling stretch band up into a diagonal pattern

# Split Squat & Shoulder Lateral Raise

🔄 5-10-15
▥ 1-2
⏱ 2-0-1 to 4-0-1

- Start in a split squat position in front of a physio ball with right lower leg on ball
- Hold a stretch band in right hand with other end firmly anchored
- Switch on your core muscles
- Do a split squat down pushing stretch band up into a lateral raise

# Split Squat & Torso Rotation

🔄 5-10-15
▥ 1-2
⏱ 2-0-1 to 4-0-1

- Start in a split squat position with a physio ball at your back
- Hold a stretch band in both hands & firmly anchored to legs
- Switch on your core muscles
- Do a split squat down as you rotate torso & arms against resistance
- Return to start position
- Repeat both sides

## Squat, Ball Squeeze & Shoulder Elevation

◷ 5-10-15
▥ 1-2
⊕ 2-0-1 to 4-0-1

Start

Finish

- Start in a squat position with a physio ball at your back
- Place a ball between knees
- Hold a stretch band in both hands firmly anchored to your thigh
- Switch on your core muscles
- Do a squat down pushing stretch band up into shoulder elevation

---

## Split Squat & Shoulder Forward Press with Ball at Side

◷ 5-10-15
▥ 1-2
⊕ 2-0-1 to 4-0-1

Start

Finish

- Start in a split squat position with a physio ball at your side
- Hold a stretch band in both hands firmly anchored to your thigh
- Switch on your core muscles
- Do a split squat down pushing stretch band out into a shoulder press
- Return to start position

# Squat, Ball Squeeze & Double Arm Diagonal Pull

↻ 5-10-15
⦀ 1-2
⏱ 2-0-1 to 4-0-1

Start

Finish

- Start in a squat position with a physio ball at your back
- Place a ball between knees
- Hold a stretch band in both hands firmly anchored under your feet
- Switch on your core muscles
- Do a squat down as you lightly squeeze ball between knees
- Do a diagonal pull with both arms as you squat down

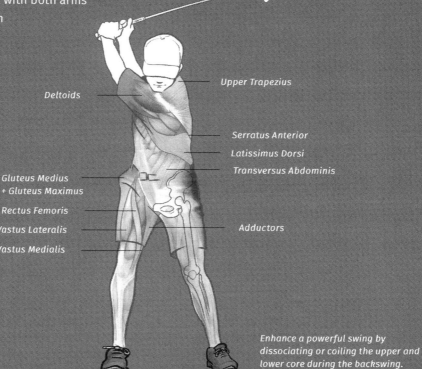

Upper Trapezius

Deltoids

Serratus Anterior

Latissimus Dorsi

Transversus Abdominis

Gluteus Medius + Gluteus Maximus

Rectus Femoris

Vastus Lateralis

Vastus Medialis

Adductors

*Enhance a powerful swing by dissociating or coiling the upper and lower core during the backswing.*

# Connect Your Core D – Knee Stability Focus

Many golfers have knee problems but most of them occur from other activities than swinging a golf club. Obviously walking the uneven terrain and hills can exacerbate pre-existing injuries.

More common is an injury from deep bending or squatting to pick up or mark a ball or from stepping in a hole or getting off the cart while it is still moving.

Older golfers can develop meniscal tears from the golf swing but usually there is predisposing joint degeneration or arthritis.

**Exercises to help improve knee function should not be painful to do. If they are see your Physician, Physiotherapist or other Primary Health Care Provider.**

# Side Lying Hip Abduction with Ball Squeeze

 5-10-15
1-2
2-0-1

*Start*

*Start ball knees*

*Start ball ankles*

- Start lying on your side with a large physio ball between knees or ankles
- Switch on your core muscles
- Raise legs up & lower slowly

---

# Supine Bridging & Hamstring Pull

 5-10
 1-2
 1-2-1

*Start*

*Middle*

*Finish*

- Start lying on your back with lower leg & feet on a physio ball
- Switch on your core muscles
- Bridge hips up & pull ball towards buttocks & hold for 2 seconds & return to start position

## Wall Squats with Ball at Back

🔄 5-10-15
Ⅲ 1-2
⏱ 2-0-1 to 4-0-1

Start

Finish

Variation

- Start standing tall with a physio ball at your back
- Switch on your core muscles
- Squat down slowly keeping knees aligned over toes & return to start position
- This exercise can be made more challenging by squeezing a ball between knees and pulling a stretch/resistance band apart with arms

---

## Sumo Squats with Ball at Back

🔄 5-10-15
Ⅲ 1-2
⏱ 2-0-1 to 4-0-1

Start

Finish

Variation

- Start standing tall in a sumo squat position with a physio ball at your back
- Switch on your core muscles
- Squat down slowly keeping knees aligned over toes & return to start position
- This exercise can be varied by using a stretch/ resistance band and doing a diagonal pull

# Single Leg Squats with Ball at Back

↻ 5-10-15
⊞ 1-2
⊕ 2-0-1 to 4-0-1

*Start*

*Finish*

*Variation*

- Start standing tall in a single leg squat position with a physio ball at your back
- Switch on your core muscles
- Do a single leg squat down slowly keeping stance knee aligned over toes & return to start position
- This exercise can be made easier by moving the back leg into a split squat position

---

# Dynamic Hip Hikes with Ball Pull Down

↻ 5-10-15 per side
⊞ 1-2
⊕ 2-0-1

*Start*

*Finish*

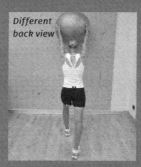
*Different back view*

- Start in a split squat position facing a wall & grasping a physio ball overhead with your hands
- Switch on your core muscles
- Drive back knee up to ball as you squeeze ball between hands & pull down
- Return to start position

## Dynamic Hip Hikes with Ball at Back

↻ 5-10-15 per side
☰ 1-2
🕐 2-0-1

- Start in a split squat position with a physio ball at your back
- Switch on your core muscles
- Drive back knee up to opposite elbow & back down slowly to start position

## Single Leg 1/4 Squat with Ball at Side

↻ 8-10-12
☰ 1-2
🕐 3-0-1

- Start standing on one leg with a physio ball at your side against a wall
- Lift inside knee to hip height
- Switch on your core muscles
- Do a single leg ¼ squat down
- Keep stance knee aligned over toes but not going past them

## Split Squat & Diagonal Torso Twist with Ball

⟳ 8-10-12
⫾ 1-2
⏱ 2-0-1

*Start*

*Finish*

*Variation*

- Start standing in a split squat position with a physio ball in your hands & held at hip height
- Switch on your core muscles
- Do a split squat as you rotate your torso taking the ball diagonally up to above shoulder
- Keep front knee aligned over toes but not going past them
- This exercise can be made easier by adopting a double leg squat position with the legs

## Split Squat & Shoulder Diagonal Pull

⟳ 5-10-15
⫾ 1-2
⏱ 2-0-1 to 4-0-1

*Start*

*Finish*

*Variation*

- Start in a split squat position in front of a physio ball with right lower leg on ball
- Hold a stretch band in right hand with other end firmly anchored
- Switch on your core muscles
- Do a split squat down pulling stretch band up into a diagonal pattern
- Another variation would be doing a lateral raise

# Connect Your Core E — Hip Stability Focus

Many injuries of the lower core and legs can originate with tension or tightness in the hips and a lack of stability and strength. These problems are exacerbated by inactivity and the seated posture.

Tight hip flexors and hamstrings (both are in shortened position while sitting) become tight and place more stress on the lower back, hip and knees. Keeping the hips flexible, strong and stable will help to protect against injury.

# Clamshell Hip Abduction

⟳ 5-10-15
▥ 1-2
⏲ 2-2-1

- Start lying on your side with both knees bent up
- Switch on your core & raise one knee up keeping ankles together – like a clam opening its shell
- Hold for 2 seconds & slowly return to start position for a 2 second count
- This exercises can be made easier by lying on your back and abducting and rotating one leg

---

# Side Lying Hip Abduction

⟳ 5-10-15
▥ 1-2
⏲ 1-2-1

- Start lying on your side with bottom knee bent & top knee straight
- Switch on your core
- Point toes down to floor on top leg & raise leg up
- Hold for 2 seconds & down slow for a 2 second count
- This exercise can be made more challenging by adding a weight to ankle/foot

## Side Lying Hip Adduction

○ 5-10-15
◫ 1-2
◷ 1-2-1

*Start*

*Finish*

*Variation*

- Start lying on your side with top knee bent & placed floor a ball or small stool
- Keep bottom knee straight
- Switch on your core & raise bottom leg up off the mat
- Hold for 2 seconds & slowly return to start position for a 2 second count

## Quadruped Bridge & Single Leg Extension with Forearms on Ball

○ 5-10-15
◫ 1-2
◷ 1-2-1

*Start*

*Finish*

*Variation*

- Start kneeling on floor with both forearms on a large physio ball
- Switch on your core muscles
- Now extend one leg out & raise up, extend leg fully & hold
- A variation would be to drive one knee forward before extending the leg

## Prone Bridge
## Feet on Ball & Walk Arms Out

↻ 5-10 / position
▥ 1-2
⏱ 1-2-1

Start    Finish    Variation

- Start in a prone push up position with lower legs on a physio ball
- Switch on your core muscles
- Walk arms out until legs straight & hold for 2 seconds then return to start position
- To make this exercise harder pull the ball towards your chest bending knees before going back to start position

## Lateral Bridging on Ball

↻ 5-10
▥ 1-2
⏱ 1-5-1 to 1-10-1

Start    Finish    Variation

- Start in a lateral bridge position with feet on floor and forearm & hand on a physio ball
- Switch on your core muscles
- Place upper hand on hips & hold for 5 to 10 seconds
- An easier variation would be starting on one knee

(Use with caution if elbow or shoulder problems)

## Lateral Bridging on Ball & Leg Lift

↻ 5-10
⦀ 1-2
⏱ 1-5-1 to 1-10-1

*Start*

*Finish*

*Variation*

- Start in a lateral bridge position with feet on floor and forearm & hand on a physio ball
- Switch on your core muscles
- Place upper hand on hips & raise upper leg into hip abduction & hold
- An easier variation would be starting on one knee

(Use with caution if elbow or shoulder problems)

---

## Split Squats
## with Ball at Back

↻ 5-10-15
⦀ 1-2
⏱ 2-0-1 to 4-0-1

*Start*

*Finish*

*Variation*

- Stand tall in a split squat position with a physio ball at your back
- Switch on your core muscles
- Do a split squat down slowly keeping knees aligned over toes & return to start position
- This exercise can be made more challenging by placing one foot on a balance pod (unstable base) and doing a rowing motion with a stretch/resistance band

# Single Leg Squat & Resisted Shoulder Flexion

- ⟳ 8-10-12
- ▥ 1-2
- ⏱ 2-0-1

 *Start*
 *Finish*
 *Variation*

- Start standing on one leg with other foot crossed behind ankle & a physio ball in your hands
- Switch on your core muscles
- Do a single leg squat slowly while you raise the ball above your head & lower slowly
- Keep stance knee aligned over toes but not going past them
- This exercises can be made easier by moving the back leg into a split squat position

# Sumo Squat & Double Arm Raise

- ⟳ 5-10-15
- ▥ 1-2
- ⏱ 2-0-1 to 4-0-1

 *Start*
 *Finish*
 *Variation*

- Start in a sumo squat position with a physio ball at your back
- Hold a stretch band in both hands firmly anchored under your feet
- Switch on your core muscles
- Do a sumo squat down as you do a lateral raise with both arms
- Another variation would be holding the stretch/resistance bands on the same side and doing an arm raise

## Chapter 7

**Medicine Ball Drills to Improve Your Game**

Using a medicine ball to perform multi core and multi planar exercises will augment your stability and improve flexibility.

Fig. 7.1   Fig. 7.2

Assisted squats 2 x 10 reps

Fig. 7.3   Fig. 7.4

Challenge balance by doing 2 x 10 leg swings (front-to-back) and (side-to-side).

# Medicine Ball Drills to Improve Your Game

The golf swing requires explosive acceleration and dynamic deceleration in a controlled and balanced motion. The medicine ball is a very useful, enjoyable and versatile piece of equipment that can be used in general athletic preparation and in golf specific drills. It gives the golfing athlete the ability to perform multi-core and multi-planar exercises from slow to higher speeds and is a great tool to augment strength training and flexibility. Stronger more supple muscles allows for a faster swing with more stability, balance and control of the club. Medicine balls provide the athletes and therapists a low-cost and portable training tool available in a wide range of weights and sizes. Europeans have an expression that "one who uses the medicine ball does not need medicine!"

Following is a selection of medicine ball exercises that can be used in developing your general fitness and conditioning or for the more golf spe-

cific strength and power components. These exercises will prove to be good medicine for golfers. It is important to consider the age and stage of development of the players involved when selecting the size and weight of the medicine balls – ideally they should range from 1 lb (1/2 kg) to 12 lb (5 kg). With a large number of exercises and variations it is simple to create training sessions that are continually challenging, interesting and effective. With the medicine ball it is also possible to do agility and mobility exercises, develop deceleration and acceleration strength and power. One can also do throwing exercises as well as games, relays and competitions that will have a beneficial effect on the athlete's general fitness.

The new types of medicine balls are made of durable rubber and bounce comfortably. This allows you to train by yourself by bouncing on the ground or against appropriate walls when throwing them. Because of the large

Fig. 7.5    Fig. 7.6    Fig. 7.7

*Warm up for rotational strength by doing 2 x 10 torso twists to each side.*

combination of exercises and different variations depending on extra equipment it is simple to create training sessions that are challenging, different, interesting, effective and golf specific enough to guarantee fitness improvement.

## GENERAL WARM-UP

Do these simple warm-up exercises before starting any of your medicine ball training sessions. These exercises help lubricate the under surface of the knee cap (patella), so it slides smoothly and tracks properly. They as well challenge your balance in different planes of motion and have you actively switching on your core muscles (see Chapter 3 "Dynamic Warm-Up" for more info). *See Fig. 7.1 – 7.7*

You can choose 2 or 3 different med ball exercises to add to your current workout or choose one of the workouts below depending on what you want to work on.

- Always warm up first.
- Start slow and progress gradually.
- When doing squats don't allow your knees to go past your toes (this increases pressure to the under surface of the knee cap).
- Focus on proper technique (ask a knowledgeable fitness or health professional if you are unsure).
- When bending and rotating remember to use as many joints as possible.
- Perform exercises in a controlled manner.
- Choose 2-3 exercises from each program for each session and change them regularly.
- Start doing 1-2 sets of 5-10-15 repetitions and as strength and stability improves increase to 2-3 sets of 10-15-20 repetitions.

Choose a medicine ball that is appropriate for you. A medicine ball weighing 2-3 kilos (4-7 lbs.) is appropriate for most adults. Adolescents should supervised and use a volleyball or basketball before progressing to a medicine ball.

Fig. 7.8 — Fig. 7.9 — Fig. 7.10 — Fig. 7.11 — Fig. 7.12 — Fig. 7.13 — Fig. 7.14 — Fig. 7.15 — Fig. 7.16 — Fig. 7.17 — Fig. 7.18

## MEDICINE BALL TRAINING PROGRAM A (ALIGNMENT STRENGTH & STABILITY)

1) Single Leg Balance 747 *(Fig. 7.8)*
2) Squats with Med Ball Arm Extension *(Fig. 7.9 / 7.10)*
3) Split Squat & Med Ball Arm Extension *(Fig. 7.11 / 7.12)*
4) Step Ups & Med Ball Arm Extension *(Fig. 7.13 / 7.14)*
5) Lateral Hops over ½ Foam Roll – or other obstacle *(Fig. 7.15 / 7.16)*
6) Bent Over Med Ball Throws *(Fig. 7.17/7.18)*

## MEDICINE BALL TRAINING PROGRAM B (BALANCE STRENGTH & STABILITY)

1) Balance on a balance pod or other unstable base *(Fig. 7.19 / 7.20)*
2) Squats squeezing a ball between knees with Med Ball Arm Extension *(Fig. 7.21 / 7.22)*
3) Split Squats & Med Ball Arm Extension on balance pod or other unstable base *(Fig. 7.23 / 7.24)*
4) Step Ups with Rotation *(Fig. 7.25 / 7.26)*
5) Step Hop Ups *(Fig. 7.27 / 7.28)*
6) Side Lunge with Rotation *(Fig. 7.29 / 7.30)*

Fig. 7.31  Fig. 7.32  Fig. 7.33  Fig. 7.34
Fig. 7.35  Fig. 7.36  Fig. 7.37  Fig. 7.38
Fig. 7.39  Fig. 7.40  Fig. 7.41  Fig. 7.42

## MEDICINE BALL TRAINING PROGRAM C (CONNECTED CORE STRENGTH & STABILITY)

1) Med Ball Seated Rotations *(Fig. 7.31 / 7.32)*
2) Single Leg Squat & Med Ball Arm Extension *(Fig. 7.33 / 7.34)*
3) Med Ball Leg Extension and Arm Deceleration Control (Fig. 7.35 / 7.36)
4) Med Ball Step Ups with Diagonal Med Ball Arm Extension *(Fig. 7.37 / 7.38)*
5) Med Ball Overhead Throws *(Fig. 7.39 / 7.40)*
6) Med Ball Side Lunge Throws *(Fig. 7.41 / 7.42)*

*A sound golf swing requires upper and lower core separation.*

These exercises are not exhaustive and you may add others based on your experience or on the advice of your health or fitness professional.

In golfers, the abdominal musculature plays a significant role in trunk and core stability providing a mechanical link between the lower core and legs and upper core and arms as you create separation during the takeaway and backswing. Medicine ball drills will help augment the core muscles and ensure a smooth transition when making a full swing. *See Fig. 7.43-7.49*

The rotational nature of the golf swing places a large amount of stress on the soft tissues (muscles, joint capsule and tendons) as you accelerate and decelerate the club in a diagonal pattern. It requires both sides of the body to work but in an asymmetrical nature leading to repetition stress and potential injury if not addressed in the training program.

Separation (a.k.a. dissociation, rotation or torque) between the lower core and upper core is a key in any sport where you use the hips to transfer forces to create arm speed. Medicine ball drills will help facilitate and augment this motion. The golf swing is produced through a kinetic chain of sequential activation of body segments from the ground to the arm, hand and club. Doing these medicine ball drills will help to coordinate your creation of force and transfer and funnel it efficiently along the chain.

VARIETY IS ONE KEY TO SUCCESS IN FOLLOWING A SMART GOLF TRAINING. IF YOU BECOME BORED, TRY CHANGING THE EXERCISES EACH FEW WEEKS.

## Chapter 8

**Cross Training for Golfers**

*Use a variety of cross training exercises in different venues to improve performance both on and off the course.*

| Borg Scale of Perceived Exertion | | Talk Test Guidelines |
|:---:|:---|:---|
| 0 | Nothing at all | Can very easily carry on a conversation |
| 1 | Very easy | |
| 2 | Easy | |
| 3 | Moderate | You should be able to carry on a conversation |
| 4 | Somewhat Hard | |
| 5 | Hard | |
| 6 | | Cannot talk continuously |
| 7 | Very Hard | |
| 8 | | Cannot talk at all |
| 9 | | |
| 10 | Very, Very Heavy (Maximal) | |

Fig. 8.1
Rate of Perceived Exertion (Borg Scale, 1982)

Fig. 8.2
Easy warm-up running

# Cross Training for Golfers (45-55 Minutes Fitness)

We all know that being in good shape will improve our golf performance, make playing more enjoyable and protect against injuries. Unfortunately with today's hectic lifestyle it can be difficult to fit in your golf workouts on a regular basis.

To help you reach your goals we have designed several quick 45-55 minute workouts that require little equipment but will help augment your stamina, balance, core-stability, deceleration strength and most importantly improve golf performance.

- All you need is running gear, a stretch band and 45–55 minutes free time.

- You can change it up by varying the route you run and use beach or forest trails to soften the impact and boost your psyche.

- Take a friend along to encourage compliance.

- In inclement weather take it inside and use a treadmill, stationary bike, stair climber or elliptical trainer instead of the running portion.

Fig. 8.3

Fig. 8.4

Fig. 8.5

High knees keep you quick on your feet and switches on your core.

Keep knees aligned over toes.

High knee drive crossover run.

## WORKOUT A – 45 MINUTE FITNESS

| 1–5 Minutes: | Warm-Up |
|---|---|
| 6–20 Minutes: | Aerobic Work |
| 21–25 Minutes: | Strength Work |
| 26–35 Minutes: | Aerobic Work |
| 36–45 Minutes: | Strength, Cool down & Stretch |

Begin with a **slow warm-up jog** for 5 minutes that includes some **dynamic mobility exercises** such as high knees, arm circles, crossover runs, backwards running, side shuffle steps and skipping. These exercises improve agility and coordination at the same time as warming up the muscles of the shoulder girdle, hips and pelvis. *See Fig. 8.2 / 8.3*

Do some **continuous running** until you reach the 20 minute mark, keeping your heart rate at between 65-75% of maximum [maximum heart rate = 220 - your age] or at a RPE (rate of perceived exertion) of a 6-7 out of 10. *See Fig. 8.1*

This ensures that you get a good aerobic benefit. Next do alternating sets of **mini squats and high knee drive crossover run**.

**Mini Squats** are very functional and provide both concentric (shortening) and eccentric (lengthening) muscle contractions. They stimulate the medial quadriceps to work and strengthening them helps maintain proper knee (over toes) alignment and may decrease knee pain that is associated with muscular imbalances. *See Fig. 8.4*

Alternate these with sets of **high knee drive crossover run**. High knee drive crossover runs improves flexibility in the hip flexors and extensors, improves balance and co-ordination in the hip, knee and ankle and increases strength in the hips and legs. Keeping your back straight and head up, do a cross over run driving one knee up and across the hips. This works on the rotational and deceleration strength needed to

Fig. 8.6

Fig. 8.7

Fig. 8.8

Sit downs

Toe raises

Push-ups

improve power in your swing. Start slowly with 2-3 sets of 5-10 repetitions and gradually increase over a month's period until you can do sets of 15-20 repetitions per side. *See Fig. 8.5*

Continue **jogging** until you reach the 35 minute mark, then start walking to cool down. While cooling down, add a little more **general body strength** to the workout by alternating different exercises.

**Alternate exercises:** Move from one exercise to the next without resting to continue the aerobic benefits.

**Sit Downs:** Work your core functionally by starting in a sit up position and doing a reverse crunch or sit down.
*See Fig. 8.6*

**Toe raises** work all lower leg muscles. Raise up slowly, hold for 2 seconds, and lower slowly. Try for 2 x 10–20. *See Fig. 8.7*

**Push-ups** improve shoulder girdle strength. *See Fig. 8.8*

Do one set of push-ups in each of three different hand positions: hands narrow (thumbs touching), hands shoulder width and hands wider than shoulders. When starting out try doing them in a kneeling position or against a table to decrease the resistance to start.

Now the forty five minutes are up and the workout is finished. Head for the showers and still have time for a quick lunch or to make dinner. Add some variety by changing the agility type exercises you do at the beginning, changing the cardio (aerobic) component from cycle to stairclimb or elliptical trainer or by changing the general body exercises.

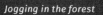

Fig. 8.9      Fig. 8.10      Fig. 8.11

Jogging in the forest    Crossover run      Leg swings front & back & side to side

## WORKOUT B – 55 MINUTE FITNESS

| | |
|---|---|
| 1–5 Minutes: | Warm-Up |
| 6–20 Minutes: | Aerobic Short Intervals Work |
| 21–25 Minutes: | Strength & Balance Work |
| 26–40 Minutes: | Aerobic Work |
| 41–55 Minutes: | Strength, Cool down & Stretch |

Start with a fast walk or walk-run for 5 minutes that includes some dynamic warm-up exercises such as arm circles, crossover runs, leg swings, high heels drills and skipping. These exercises improve agility, balance, coordination and speed (ABC's) that are important for all sports activities at the same time as warming up the muscles of the shoulder girdle, hips and pelvis. *See Fig. 8.9 / 8.10 / 8.11*

Run alternating one minute fast and one minute slower in intervals until you reach the 20 minute mark. This ensures that you get a good aerobic boost if done at a moderate intensity rate of perceived exertion (RPE) for the fast run 7-8 on a 10 point scale and for the slower run at a 3-5. *See Fig. 8.1*

Now do some balance exercises standing on an unstable surface. Balance is a fundamental component of functional mobility and dynamic activity and should be part of the daily training routine. Working on balance training is important for golfers as you increase strength because you want to continually reset the balance clock. Challenge your balance, stability and strength by adopting different balance poses on the uneven surface of a log, rock or bench. *See Fig. 8.12 / 8.13*

Though little research has been done to date, data suggests that using a variety of unstable rather than stable surfaces will activate the trunk (core) muscles more, especially on exercises that are unilateral (one-sided) in nature like golf. A practical application of this would be

*Fig. 8.12*

*Different balance poses on a log*

*Fig. 8.13*

*Hurdler high knee lifts*

stand on a surface that is uneven or unstable like a log or on a piece of balance equipment like a wobble board or balance disc in the gym setting.

Continue jogging or other aerobic activity of choice until the 45 minute mark, then start walking to cool down. During your cool down do strength exercises that focus in on leg and core strength. Do the exercises slowly especially on the deceleration portion to improve hip and leg strength. Move from one exercise to the next without resting to continue the workout benefits. Do 2-3 sets of 10-20 repetitions or until the 55 minutes are up.

*See Fig. 8.14 / 8.15 / 8.16 / 8.17 / 8.18 / 8.19*

Half Squats A & B

Lateral lunges

Hip flexion with torso rotation

Tricep dips

Sit downs work the abdominal eccentrically.

Hip bridges

Fig. 8.20    Fig. 8.21

High knee balance drills    Airplane balance drills

Fig. 8.22

Squats with diagonal cord pull

## WORKOUT C – 55 MINUTE FITNESS

| | |
|---|---|
| 1–5 Minutes: | Warm-Up |
| 6–20 Minutes: | Aerobic Work |
| 21–25 Minutes: | Balance Work |
| 26–40 Minutes: | Aerobic Work |
| 41–55 Minutes: | Strength, Cool down & Stretch |

Start with a **slow jog or other aerobic activity** for 5 minutes that includes some dynamic warm-up exercises such as arm circles, crossover runs, high knees, backwards running, side shuffle steps and skipping. These exercises improve agility, balance, coordination and speed (ABC's) that are important for all sports activities including golf at the same time as warming up the muscles of the shoulder girdle, hips and pelvis. *See Fig. 8.9 - 8.11*

**Run continuously** until you reach the 18-20 minute mark, keeping your heart rate at between 65-75% of maximum [maximum heart rate = 220

- your age] or working at a 6-7 out of 10 on the Borg Scale (rate of perceived exertion). *See Fig. 8.20.* This ensures that you get a good aerobic benefit since evidence suggests we need at least 30 (up to 60) minutes of moderate intensity exercise on most if not all days of the week.

Now do some hip and balance warm-up exercises standing on an unstable surface. Always keep your core switched on like a dimmer switch on a light. Do some balance drills try standing on a log on one leg with knee up to 90 degrees and arms held in front to challenge your balance and stand on one leg and go into an airplane position with one leg back and arms out in front and hold for 5-10 seconds and repeat 2-3 times each leg. *See Fig. 8.20 / 8.21*

Continue jogging or other aerobic activity of choice until the 40 minute mark, then start walking to cool down. During your cool down do

Fig. 8.23

*Step ups with shoulder rotation*

Fig. 8.24

*Sumo squats with X band*

strength exercises that focus in on lower extremity stability and strength. Do the exercises slowly especially on the deceleration portion to improve specific strength. Move from one exercise to the next without resting to continue the workout benefits.

Exercises like step-ups and squats can be designed to be more functional and work both the upper and lower core by adding elastic tubing. This achieves a good balance of stress for the body's upper and lower extremities and three-dimensional core cylinder. Exercises should be done in a slow and controlled, coordinated, and functional manner. Work on deceleration control by going slower during the eccentric (lengthening) phase of the exercise to make the exercises more challenging.

Stand with one end of your light stretch/resistance band under one foot. Do a partial squat while pulling the cord into a diagonal pattern.

Do 2 sets of 10-20 repetitions.
*See Fig. 8.22*

Place one foot on a step and hold your light stretch band in your hands. As you step up externally rotate the shoulders against the resistance of the band. Do 2 sets of 10-20 repetitions. *See Fig. 8.23*

Stand with feet shoulder width apart, toes pointed out and a light stretch band under your feet and held at waist level with hands together. Do 2 sets of 10-20 repetitions of a sumo squat raising the arms into an overhead position. Keep knees tracking in line with your toes. *See Fig. 8.24*

Now the 55 minutes are up. Hit the shower and still have time to spare. Add variety by changing the agility exercises you do at the beginning, changing the cardio (aerobic) component from cycle to stair climb or elliptical trainer or by

*Fig. 8.25*    *Fig. 8.26*    *Fig. 8.27*    *Fig. 8.28*

*Quadriceps stretch*    *Hip flexor stretch*    *Seated gluteal stretch*    *Hamstring stretch*

changing the general body exercises. By using a variety of exercises or drills that incorporate balance and functional kinetic chain exercises for the lower and upper body make sessions more enjoyable and athletes less likely to become stale and bored. It is important to prevent boredom and to maximize the potential for improvement.

A couple of things to remember: first, if you have any doubts about your current fitness level, consult a physician before beginning this or any other exercise program. Secondly, stretches for all muscles groups should be part of your post training routine. Past research shows that static stretches prior to exercise did not prevent lower extremity overuse injuries, but additional static stretches after training and before bed resulted in 50 percent fewer injuries. Take stretches to the point of tension not pain and hold for 30 seconds – repeating 2-3 times.
*See Fig. 8.25 / 8.26 / 8.27 / 8.28*

# Workout Tips

Maintaining general fitness between workouts is easy if you follow a few simple tips. Develop a 'fit' attitude. Keep moving should be your philosophy.

• Walk to the store or a friend's house.
• Get off the bus early and walk the last 10 minutes to and from work.
• Take the stairs instead of the elevator.
• Use hot and cold showers for the regenerative effect on the tissues.

## Chapter 9

## Smart Stretching Guidelines

# Stretch your limits to become a better golfer.

Fig. 9.1

Standing hip flexor stretch

Fig. 9.2

Latissimus dorsi stretch

Fig. 9.3

Forearm stretch

# Smart Stretching Guidelines

How often have you heard golfers comment, "My hips are stiff and my back is sore. What should I do?" Well, the answer is stretch. Unfortunately, when time comes at a premium, the first thing to go is often the most boring – stretching. But stretching is important, not only to keep the body moving well promoting a healthy swing, but also to prevent injury and aid recovery from training. Tight muscles are slow muscles and impair the speed and feel of your swing. Normally, the muscles and tendon complexes will act as mini-shock absorbers for the joints. However, if they are short and stiff, the shock absorption capabilities are decreased, leading to stress on other areas of the kinetic chain. A smooth and efficient swing requires good functional flexibility and optimum joint mobility (range of motion).

Try doing some conform, slow static, and facilitated/partner stretches to optimize muscle and tendon length post training. Golfers should develop, with the aid of a physical trainer or physiotherapist, a static stretching routine that is performed consistently and comprises at least 8-10 exercises.

## WHIRLPOOL STRETCHES

One way to do this is to stretch while on the phone or computer or when in the swimming pool, sauna or whirlpool. *See Fig. 9.1 / 9.2 / 9.3* Prior to stretching it is important to prepare by raising your body temperature and increasing circulation. Doing some large muscle activity like climbing stairs, fast walk, jog, skipping or cycling will achieve this.

**The three types of stretching in this chapter:**
- Conform Stretching
- Slow Static Stretching (Lower & Upper Body)
- Facilitated/Partner Stretching

Fig. 9.4
Iliotibial band/hip abductors & lateral flexors torso

Fig. 9.5
Hamstring & forearm extensors

Fig. 9.6
Calf (gastrocnemius) & latissimus dorsi

Fig. 9.7
Hip adductor & posterior shoulder

Fig. 9.8
Seated gluteals & foreams

Fig. 9.9
Standing hip flexor & triceps

Fig. 9.10
Standing gastrocnemius & pectorals

## CONFORM STRETCHING (PRE-ACTIVITY)

While research suggests that prolonged static stretching is not appropriate prior to activity, conform stretches that are easy, controlled, low range of motion moving stretches that take the muscles and joints through a comfortable range of motion are appropriate. They are not aggressive enough to tear or aggravate muscle fibers that are already shortened or injured due to hard exercise. Conform stretches are best done imme-diately before or after exercise and held only for 15–20 seconds as part of the gradual warm-up or cool down.

## CONFORM STRETCHING (POST-TRAINING)

Continued movement and light stretching after training are important to minimize DOMS (delayed onset muscle soreness) and reduce the potential for injury. Muscle soreness is believed

Fig. 9.11

Pectoral

Fig. 9.12 Fig. 9.13

Back (double knee to chest)    Back (single knee to chest)

Fig. 9.14    Fig. 9.15

Low back and hip abductors    Figure 4 or pretzel stretch

Fig. 9.16

Standing hip flexor and quadriceps stretch.

to be decreased with mild stretching exercises performed during the cool down period (Prentice, 1983). Conform stretching exercises should be done as part of a regular routine. Now is not the time to try to aggressively stretch tight, knotted muscles. Instead, take the stretch to easy tension and hold for 15–20 seconds or move slowly through the stretch causing the muscle fibers to slide. Be systematic, stretching all major muscle groups. This includes leg muscles of the quadriceps, hamstrings, calf, back,

abductors, and adductors. Exhale as you move through the stretch then breathe normally.

For some athletes, doing 10 different stretches may be too time consuming on a daily basis; therefore, choosing stretches that are multi-muscle and multi-joint can maximize stretching effectiveness while minimizing time spent.

*See Fig. 9.4 – 9.10*

Fig. 9.17 / Fig. 9.18 / Fig. 9.19 / Fig. 9.20

Hamstring stretch    Quadriceps stretch    Standing hip flexor stretch    Seated hip adductor stretch

Fig. 9.21    Fig. 9.22

Standing hip adductor stretch    Seated figure 4 gluteal stretch

**MANY SHORT STRETCHES THROUGHOUT THE DAY ARE BETTER THAN DOING NONE.**

Be sure to key in on those that tend to get short and stiff like the hamstrings, hip flexors, calves and pectorals as well as the decelerators like the quadriceps and posterior shoulder.

Conform stretches should also be performed for the shoulders and elbows. Stretch the forearm extensors and flexors. Stretch each muscle group to the point of tension not pain.

Chest (pectoral) stretch can be done by placing an arm against a wall or secure object and stretching shoulder forward to feel a pull in the anterior chest. *See Fig. 9.11*

Be patient when it comes to improving your flexibility because significant gains can only be realized after several weeks or months of consistent work.

# Smart Stretching Guidelines

Fig. 9.23          Fig. 9.24          Fig. 9.25          Fig. 9.26

Forearm extensor stretch    Forearm flexor stretch    Forearm & hand stretch    Tricep stretch

After training follow the **high performance recovery tips and strategies** in Chapter 11.

## SLOW, STATIC STRETCHING

This type of stretching should be done daily after a proper warm-up (achieve a light sweat-under arms damp) and during the cool-down period after training. If you're running late, stretch at home while text messaging or watching television. Utilize a variety of stretching types to optimize your flexibility gains. Research indicates that stretches prior to exercise did not prevent lower extremity overuse injuries, but additional static stretches after training and before bed resulted in 50 percent fewer injuries (Hartig and Henderson, 1999). Therefore save the aggressive static stretching for after the training session and during the rules of recovery for golfers (see Chapter 11). Try holding each stretch for a minimum of 30 seconds and repeat 2-3 times. Ensure you review the dynamic warm-up sections which outline the exercises that should be done before training and before golfing.

Slow, static stretching is best done as a separate session after your training or round is over and after you have warmed up the core temperature and muscles with an activity like cycle, elliptical trainer, fast walking or a swimming pool warm-up.

## LOWER BODY STRETCHES

Most static stretches should be held for 30 seconds and repeated 2–3 times; however, more significant gains in flexibility will be made if the stretches are held longer than one minute and repeated 3–4 times (most athletes told to stretch for one minute do 30 seconds). It takes at least 20–30 seconds to overcome the bias from the protective stretch reflex. Stretch the tightest areas first. Be progressive in your stretching.

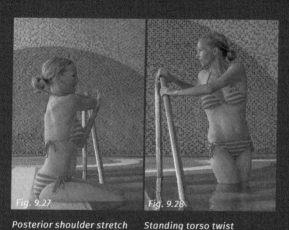

Fig. 9.27
*Posterior shoulder stretch*

Fig. 9.28
*Standing torso twist*

Fig. 9.29
*Standing lateral trunk stretches*

Exhale as you stretch further into the range, and then breathe normally as the stretch is held at the point of tension or tightness. The state of tension in other muscle groups should be assessed on a daily basis and new stretches added to ensure that a good length-tension relationship is maintained in all muscle groups responsible for off and on course performance. *See Fig. 9.12 – 9.22*

Stretches can also be done while sitting on a physio (stability) ball. By supporting your weight seated or leaning on the ball you allow the muscles you are trying to stretch to relax.

## UPPER BODY STRETCHES

### Key Areas

- Focus on muscles that tend to be relatively short and stiff. This includes the pectorals, hip flexors, hamstrings, hip adductors, and calf muscles.

- Work with your physical therapist or strength and conditioning coach to determine which stretches are best for you. *See Fig. 9.23–9.29*

## FACILITATED/PARTNER STRETCHING

### Hold-Relax and Contact-Relax

While static stretching has been the most widely researched, other stretching techniques such as PNF (proprioceptive neuromuscular facilitation), conform, and myofascial (or pressure point release) are all helpful. Facilitated partner stretches such as hold-relax and contract-relax PNF techniques have been shown to be more effective than just static stretching (Lucas & Koslow, 1984) (Enoka, 1994). PNF techniques can be more relaxing, as you can lie down and be stretched passively while performing minimal work.

Facilitated stretches make use of the "inverse myotatic reflex", where nerve receptors in the tendon are sensitive to isometric contraction and relax the muscle when it occurs.

# Smart Stretching Guidelines

Fig. 9.30

*PNF hip flexor stretch*

Fig. 9.31

*PNF hamstring stretch*

**Two methods may be used:**
- Contract-Relax: tighten the same (agonist) muscle, then stretch.
- Hold-Relax: tighten the opposite (antagonist) muscle, then stretch.

Many traditional static stretches can also become facilitated stretches by using a resistance band, rope, towel, tree, wall, or your hands to apply resistance. This type of stretching will help increase range of motion and strengthen the muscle. Have your physical therapist or fitness coach help you with these.
*See Fig. 9.30 – 9.33*

## FIT TO PLAY GOLF-TRAINING TIPS

- If a particular stretching exercise causes discomfort, try an alternative one or decrease the tension used.

- Include one stretch for each major muscle group targeted for the stretching session.

- If particular muscle groups are stiff, such as the hip flexors or iliotibial band, stretch them first and last.

- Allow a minimum of 10–15 minutes for a dynamic warm-up prior to stretching.

- A more comprehensive warm-up and static and facilitated partner stretching session will take from 30–60 minutes.

- If cycling is the training activity, be sure to stretch the lateral quadriceps and iliotibial band twice as much as you usually do.

Fig. 9.32

*PNF adductor stretch*

Fig. 9.33

*PNF gluteals stretch*

# Rules of Stretching

- Do a warm-up prior to any type of stretching.
- Do a dynamic warm-up to prepare for any activity, including golfing.
- Do stretch dynamically before each and every training session.
- Do conform stretches after hard exercise.
- Do establish optimal sport-specific range of motion prior to the season starting.
- Do self-monitor optimal range of motion regularly.
- Do utilize a separate time and routine for static stretching 4–6 times per week, waiting several hours after hard exercise to do them.
- Do use a small ball or foam roll to help stretch tight muscles, especially if away traveling and no therapists are available.
- Do take one day off from stretching per week.
- Use a combination of the different types of stretching to develop your own personal stretching routine.

## Chapter 10

**Soft Tissue Release with Small Ball**

Add suppleness to your body and distance to your game with these soft tissue release techniques.

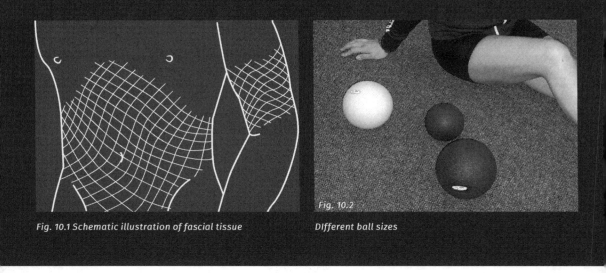

Fig. 10.1 Schematic illustration of fascial tissue

Fig. 10.2

Different ball sizes

# Soft Tissue Release with Small Ball (Muscle and Fasciae)

The myofascial system has received increased attention in the past few years. This intricate system surrounds all the muscles, nerves, and blood vessels in the body. It is a complex web-like system that separates muscles into compartments. Dysfunction in this system is common. Because this system wraps around each muscle fibril in the body, it can become twisted and snagged in different places. It is like a nylon stocking surrounding your muscles, and with dysfunction, this stocking can become caught or tight in certain places.
See Fig. 10.1

Physiotherapists, massage therapists, and other health professionals have been suggesting to patients to use their hands, tennis balls, foam rollers, and other implements to release sore, tight muscle and fascial tissue for years. Myo-

fascial release refers to a group of techniques used to relieve soft tissue from the abnormal grip of tight fascia (Juett, 1988). Myofascial release is not a new concept—Dr. Janet Travell documented many techniques in the 1940s. In addition to these techniques small rubber, myofascial release balls are being used to stretch and soften tight muscles (Soleway, 2001). These balls work not only to release trigger points in the muscle but also can work to "smooth out" the myofascial system and decrease delayed onset muscle soreness.

The effectiveness of massage or soft tissue techniques as an adjunct to stretching in order to facilitate flexibility have been demonstrated in the past (Witkorson-Moller, 1983). Physiotherapists use manual techniques to help decrease trigger points that are defined by Travell and

Simons as an exquisitely tender point in a taut band of muscle (Travell & Simons, 1998). Active, irritable trigger points that result from heavy training may reduce muscle strength and inhibit the normal contraction-relaxation coordination of the muscles. Obviously, this will not be conducive to pain free training. These problems can impair training and competition and can progress to injury if they are not resolved (Brukner & Khan, 2002).

Small ball body rolling is a great way to stretch and release tight muscles. The concept is very simple: Use the ball to "iron out" tight areas. By rolling on the ball along the muscle and at different angles to the muscle, you are trying to "untwist" the myofascial system. The aim of this technique is to induce a prolonged lengthening of tissue as distinct from a stretch, which may or may not lead to a long-term change (Granter, 2002). If an area is especially tight or sensitive, use the ball as a trigger point release tool and stay on the sore spot (Soleway, 2001). The fascia system seems to respond best when gentle pressure is applied and sustained for more than two minutes. This will help stimulate the tension receptors, induce relaxation, create analgesic response, and deactivate trigger points (Brukner & Khan, 2002).

This chapter shows soft tissue release techniques using a variety of sizes of rubber balls. But, one can also use a tennis ball, foam roll or other implements to do a similar soft tissue release.

## CHOOSE THE RIGHT SIZE BALL

Myofascial release balls come in 3 or 4 sizes. The larger the ball, the easier it is to roll on and the more comfortable it should be. The smallest of the balls either a (3-5–inch diameter) is less comfortable to roll on and is typically used once the person is more experienced with rolling. *See Fig. 10.2*

## PRECAUTIONS AND CONTRAINDICATIONS*

Ball rolling and other types of muscle and fascial release techniques are not appropriate for everyone. Be careful with certain body areas or medical conditions.

### Caution areas
- Tailbone
- Floating ribs (11 and 12)
- Lower tip of the breastbone
- Upper neck and mid-neck
- Over the hip bone (bursae sac)

### Conditions and diseases not appropriate for small ball rolling
- Malignancy
- Fractures
- Systemic or localized infections
- Open wounds or stitches
- Acute rheumatoid arthritis
- Osteoporosis

(* adapted after Soleway, 2001)

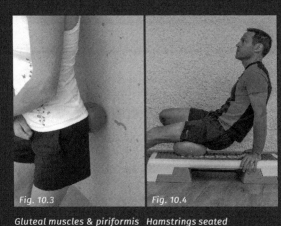

Fig. 10.3  Fig. 10.4

Gluteal muscles & piriformis   Hamstrings seated

Fig. 10.5

Calf seated

## GETTING STARTED

Use the ball and simply roll along or across muscles that need to be stretched. Keep in mind that a tight muscle is rarely an isolated case. For example, if you have a tight iliotibial band, it is likely that your hamstrings, quadriceps, and gluteal muscles will also be tight, so use the ball along many muscles to get maximal benefit.

Rolling around the pelvis is important as it is the attachment site for numerous muscles. The fascia and connective tissue around the lumbar spine and the sacrum are often associated with lower body muscular dysfunction, so make sure to get to the insertion points of the muscles and tendons.

### Gluteal muscles and piriformis
- Start at the sacrum and roll out toward the hip.
- Stay on spots of increased tenderness and hold until you feel the tension release.

*See Fig. 10.3*

### Hamstrings and calf
- Roll along the length of hamstrings and calf.
- Support weight with arms.
- If you have wrist or shoulder problems that make it difficult, you can place the ball on a low bench.

*See Fig. 10.4 / 10.5 / 10.6*

### Iliotibial band and buttocks
- Roll along the length of the ITB, starting in the buttocks and rolling to the knee.
- Hold on spots of increased tenderness.
- Also move perpendicularly across the Iliotibial band and buttocks.
- If you have wrist or shoulder problems that make it difficult, you can place the ball against the wall.
- Avoid the hip bone area as there is a bursae over top of it that can be irritated with direct pressure.

*See Fig. 10.6 / 10.7*

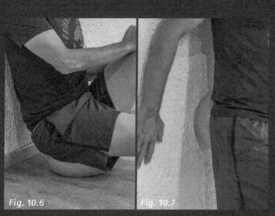

Fig. 10.6    Fig. 10.7

Iliotibial band & buttock on the floor or against the wall

Fig. 10.8

Quadriceps on the floor

Fig. 10.9

Hip adductors

Fig. 10.10

Foot rolling with a tennis ball

Fig. 10.11

Lumbar & thoracic spine

## Quadriceps

- Support weight with arms and roll down along length of muscles.
- Angle body differently to get lateral versus medial quadriceps and adductors.
- If you have wrist or shoulder problems that make it difficult, you can place the ball on a low bench.

See Fig. 10.8

## Hip Adductors

- Support weight with arms and roll down along length of muscles.
- Use a phone book or block under the ball to allow more pressure to be applied.
- Angle body differently to get to different parts of the adductors.

See Fig. 10.9

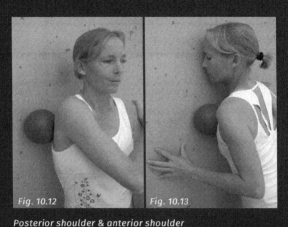

Fig. 10.12   Fig. 10.13   Fig. 10.14   Fig. 10.15   Fig. 10.16

*Posterior shoulder & anterior shoulder*          *Forearm & upper arm (wall)*

## Foot

- Step and roll on the ball to massage the muscles of the foot.
- You may find a tennis ball works better.

*See Fig. 10.10*

## Lumbar and thoracic spine musculature

- Have the ball just to the outside of your spine and gently roll up and down and perpendicular to the spine.
- Roll up to the bottom of your shoulder blade.

*See Fig. 10.11*

## Posterior shoulder and anterior shoulder musculature

- Some people feel it is best to roll against a wall for the muscles of the shoulder.
- Move your arm to different angles to actively stretch the muscles at the same time as rolling.

*See Fig. 10.12 / 10.13*

## Forearm and upper arm

- Place the ball against the wall or on a table.
- Stretch out the muscles of the forearm flexors and extensors by sliding your arm back and forth on the ball.

*See Fig. 10.14 / 10.15 / 10.16*

## Cervical spine musculature

- Some people find rolling on the neck muscles too uncomfortable.
- Try a larger ball first for comfort and work the muscles and the vertebrae to soften the area.
- You can also deflate your ball a little to make it more comfortable.

Small ball release work is a fantastic way for golfers and other athletes to self-manage tight muscles and stiffened areas, especially when no professional help is available from a physiotherapist, massage therapist, trainer, or other therapist.

The balls work well for hard to stretch areas (iliotibial band) and for muscles that are prone to tightening with exercise. Limitations with the ball do exist and should not be substituted for the hands of an experienced therapist.

## Chapter 11

**Rules of Recovery for Golfers**

*Implementing the rules of recovery into your training plans will help you become a stronger, healthier and better golfer.*

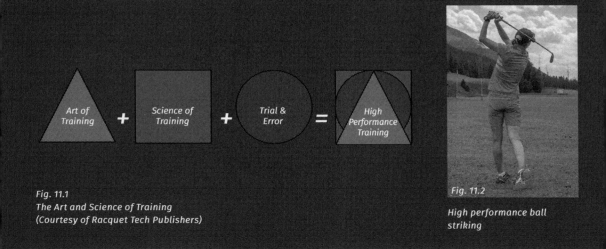

Fig. 11.1
The Art and Science of Training
(Courtesy of Racquet Tech Publishers)

Fig. 11.2
High performance ball
striking

# Rules of Recovery for Golfers

Golfers and other athletes have to be in great shape and recover well to perform on a consistent basis. They can be exposed to a demanding training schedule often training several times per day. Under these extreme circumstances they may be pushed beyond physiological and psychological norms which may result in decreased function (Bompa, 1985). Adequate recovery is a necessary part of training and important for physical, psychological and emotional health. Being only slightly under-recovered over an extended period of time results in underperformance in athletes and non-athletes alike (Kellman, 2002). Golfers often neglect using recovery techniques, therefore recovery strategies must be built into the training and tournament schedule.

Athletes, therapists and coaches must always strive to find a balance between training, competing and recovery. Some athletes train or compete when they are sick or injured and they sometimes do too much, too fast, too hard, too soon and risk problems associated with over-training or overuse injuries.

With the pressures of work, school, family and travel it is difficult to ensure proper recovery guidelines are followed after and between on and off course training.

Physical therapists and coaches who work with athletes/clients on a regular-ongoing basis can facilitate recovery by providing ideas and opportunities to utilize recovery techniques.

High performance training is a combination of art and science with some trial and error added to the mix. *See Fig. 11.1* Following is a list of 'Rules of Recovery' that athletes can do for themselves or others like physical therapists can do for athletes. Ensuring they are

*Fig. 11.3*
*Whirlpool with ice helps aid recovery.*

*Fig. 11.4*
*Hydration*

implemented on a regular basis will help facilitate recovery in both the short and long term.

## RULES OF RECOVERY

- Re-Hydrate
- Re-Fuel
- Re-Align the Body
- Recovery Work
- Release the Soft Tissue
- Regain and Maintain Muscle Length
- Re-Set the Balance Clock
- Re-Connect the Core
- Reinvigorate with Hydrotherapy
- Resynchronize during Travel

## RE-HYDRATE

Two of the most important nutritional consider-ations for recovery relates to fluid and fuel replacement strategies, therefore drink plenty of water or clear fluid. The goal is to have light colored urine. The harder, higher and hotter conditions you train or play in, the more you need to drink.

Pre-hydration and immediate re-hydration are key. Losing as little as 2% of body weight through sweat can impair an athlete's ability to perform due to low blood volume and less than optimal utilization of nutrients and oxygen. Also, younger athletes may need to be more vigilant about hydration strategies as dehydration seems to be more detrimental to children than to adults (Bar-Or, 2001). *See Fig. 11.4*

Fig. 11.5

*Doing simple self correction exercises*

Fig. 11.6

*Spinal roll stretch for lower back & gluteals*

## RE-FUEL

Golfers can minimize the effects of fatigue by starting each round with their energy/fuel tanks full. Adequate supplies of glycogen in the muscle and in the liver are needed to support the energy demands of the player and promote recovery. Ensure that adequate nutrition (carbohydrate fuel) is consumed pre and post-training. Dietary carbohydrate is the primary source for the body to manufacture glucose (Coyle, 1995). Since glycogen stores take 24-48 hours to replenish, they must be replaced daily (Costill & Hargreaves, 1992). Each gram of glycogen is stored with approximately 3 grams of water, so ensure adequate hydration to ensure maximum glycogen synthesis.

If training hard remember that there is a window of opportunity within the first 20–30 minutes after strenuous exercise, to replenish muscle fuel stores at a faster rate than if carbohydrate intake is delayed for longer. Small amounts of protein taken with carbohydrates before, during and after hard training, help minimize muscle protein breakdown as a result of heavy workloads. Athletes should consume between 1.2 and 1.5 g/kg body weight of simple carbohydrates as soon as possible after exercise (Costill & Hargreaves, 1992).

## RE-ALIGN THE BODY

Training for a sport like golf is asymmetrical in nature and can torque the body's muscle and fascial systems leading to an imbalance in length and strength of muscles and tendons. The malalignment syndrome remains one of the frontiers in medicine, unrecognized as a cause of over 50% of back and limb pain (Schamberger, 2002).

This malalignment syndrome can cause biomechanical changes – especially a shift in weight-bearing and associated asymmetries of muscle tension, strength and joint range of motion that affects soft tissues, joints and organ systems

Fig. 11.7

Fig. 11.8

Fig. 11.9

Fig. 11.10

Spinning on the stationary cycle

Easy pool running

Use high knees marching for variety in pool recovery.

Torso rotations help recovery in different planes of movement.

throughout the body. Abnormal pelvic motion during training can put undue strain on a variety of structures that lead to overuse problems in the lumbar and thoracic spine and extremities.

### Practical Application

Golfers should do a do a self-check on their alignment and do self-correction if required post training, after driving a long distance or seated travel. If they are unsure if they are malaligned they should seek the help of a qualified professional therapist and be instructed on a series of corrective stretches.
*See Fig. 11.5 / 11.6*

be used in the absence of a bike.

### Practical Application

Build a recovery routine into your training plan. Try a light cycle (use light resistance) and pedal at 85-90 RPM (revolutions per minute) and a heart rate of 100-115 beats per minute for 15-20 minutes.
*See Fig. 11.7*

Easy water running, marching, treading water and arm swings will also help flush out the waste products from the soft tissues.
*See Fig. 11.8 / 11.9 / 11.10*

## RECOVERY WORK

To help flush out the lactic acid and other waste products that built up in the muscle during training and play, try the following cycle routine "spin only". At higher pedalling rates there is a greater recruitment of slow twitch fibres. Other modalities such as pool running or walking can

## RELEASE THE SOFT TISSUE

There are many well known soft tissue techniques used in treating sports injuries including longitudinal stroking, strip and stretch or active release technique, tranverse friction, tranverse gliding, sustained myofascial tension, vibrational techniques and digital ischemic pressure.

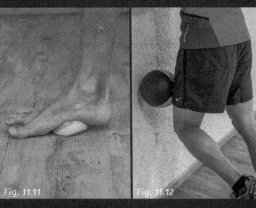

Fig. 11.11     Fig. 11.12     Fig. 11.13     Fig. 11.14

*Foot release*     *Quadriceps release*     *Quadriceps stretch*     *Hamstring stretch*

Utilizing a variety of techniques based on athletes preference and experience can help promote recovery. Depending on facilities and expertise available, the post training soft tissue work can be done either by a professional or by a training partner, parent, coach or by the athlete themselves. For example soft tissue techniques can be done on the upper and lower extremities when in the whirlpool using the pressure of the water jets.

## Practical Application

The fascia system responds best when gentle pressure is applied and sustained for two or more minutes.

Use a tennis ball to roll under foot to release the tight muscles. *See Fig. 11.11*

Quadriceps release using a small ball against a wall will decrease tension in anterior thigh muscles. *See Fig. 11.12*
See Chapter 10 (Soft Tissue Release with Small Ball) for more ideas.

## REGAIN AND MAINTAIN MUSCLE LENGTH

The state of tension in muscle groups should be assessed on a daily basis and new stretches added to ensure that a good length-tension balance is maintained in all muscle groups responsible for on and off course performance. Athletes should develop their own set of stretches based on an evaluation by their sport science and medicine team and be adjusted as the training emphasis and demands change.
*See Fig. 11.13 / 11.14*

See Chapter 9 (Smart Stretching Guidelines) for more ideas.

## RE-SET THE BALANCE CLOCK

Balance training is a fundamental component of functional mobility and dynamic sports activity and should be part of everyone's daily fitness routine whether destined for the pro-circuit or not (Petersen, 2006b). As physiotherapists and

Fig. 11.15

Fig. 11.16

*Single leg stance helps re-set the balance clock.*

*Re-set the balance clock using unstable pods with upper core exercise.*

Fig. 11.17

*Extension exercises on physio ball re-connects the core.*

fitness coaches we have long known the benefits of balance and body awareness exercises in rehabilitating injuries and in sport specific training. Fatigue associated with hard training impairs proprioceptive mechanisms and may directly trigger nociceptors (Bruker & Khan, 2002). This combination of fatigue, impaired proprioception and potential inhibition due to pain make it imperative to try and reset the joints 3-dimensional balance clock before being put in a potential injury situation.

**Practical Application**

Most gyms will have some balance equipment available. By training on an unstable surface, balance reactions and coordination are trained at a subconscious level, facilitating these reactions to become automatic. Golfers should re-set their balance clock with some drills using wobble boards, foam rolls, balance pods or simply rolled towels. You also challenge your balance simply by doing leg swings, or single leg balance with resistance bands.
*See Fig. 11.15 / 11.16*

## RE-CONNECT THE CORE

All athletes including golfers need a strong core to maintain balance, stability and alignment as they generate power in their swing. When moving in multi-planar directions, the core muscles and hip stabilizers work functionally to control movement.

**Practical Application**

Try some prone arm and leg raises over a large physio ball to re-connect the upper and lower core muscles. *See Fig. 11.17*

Try doing some double or single leg squats with a ball at your back and add some scapular retractions to re-connect the upper and lower core muscles.

As well doing squats while squeezing a ball between your knees and pulling a stretch cord apart combines the upper and lower core, the legs perform a closed kinetic chain squat as the stretch band partially closes the upper extremity

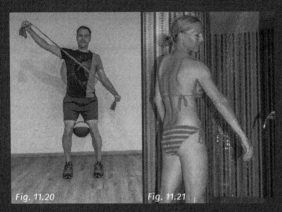

Fig. 11.18    Fig. 11.19    Fig. 11.20    Fig. 11.21

Supine ball bridge with scapular retraction

Squats squeezing ball and pulling stretch cord

Shower often to help flush the waste products

kinetic chain to improve 3 dimensional core strength. Adding a rotational component makes it more golf specific.
*See Fig. 11.18 / 11.19 / 11.20*

See Chapter 5 (Strong & Stable Platform for a Better Swing and Chapter 6 (Connecting Your Core For a Stronger Game) for more ideas.

## REINVIGORATE WITH HYDROTHERAPY MENU

Golfers and other athletes need to be aware of the importance of restoration and regeneration following heavy workloads and how to use the equipment, facilities and modalities available to facilitate recovery. These include adequate warm down, the use of whirlpools or spas and massage, as well as nutritional and psychological techniques (Brukner & Khan, 2002). By including various water based procedures such as showers (circular, pulse, needle), baths of various types including whirlpools, baths, fresh and salt waters and temperature variations like steam,

sauna, and hot-cold you can promote faster removal of waste products and may also assist in a general circulatory effect and desensitize or toughen the athlete.

### Practical Applications

### Showers
Use them to cleanse pores. Shower promptly after training to clean the skin and help flush out waste products. Remember the skin is the largest organ in the body. Repeat often – especially on hotter days.
*See Fig. 11.21*

### Suggested Contrast Temperatures
Utilizing contrast temperatures is more an art than a science and depend entirely on the facilities available to the athlete. Below are some suggested routines that over the years have worked well to re-invigorate athletes and coaches alike. Use steam rooms, ice, cold pools, whirlpools or other water based modalities available to you.

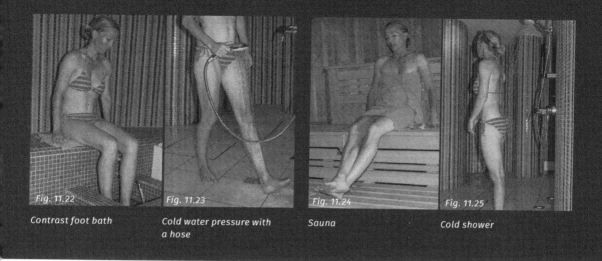

Fig. 11.22     Fig. 11.23     Fig. 11.24     Fig. 11.25

*Contrast foot bath*     *Cold water pressure with a hose*     *Sauna*     *Cold shower*

Hot & Cold (A)

- Hot (comfortable) for 2 minutes followed by cold (as possible) for 10 seconds and repeat 6 to 10 times.

Hot & Cold (B)

- Cold (as able to stand) for 1 minute followed by hot (as comfortable) for 30 seconds repeat 8 to 10 times.

*See Fig. 11.22*

Water Pressure (Hose)

- Cold water hose applied for 45 seconds to each leg and 30 seconds to each arm followed by a warm shower for 30 seconds each leg and 20 seconds each arm. Repeat 5 to 7 times.

*See Fig. 11.23*

**Sauna/Cold Plunge** (use at least one hour after training)

Start with a warm to cool shower for 3 to 5 minutes and then towel dry. Use the sauna for approximately 7 minutes at a temperature of 80–90 degrees centigrade. Follow this with a cold plunge or cold shower for 15 to 30 seconds then rest with feet up for 5 minutes. This routine can be repeated three times before a day off playing or training and repeat one time before a hard training or a tournament day. Finish with warm shower for three to five minutes.

*See Fig. 11.24 / 11.25*

### RESYNCHRONIZE DURING TRAVEL

High performance golfing athletes travel often and the cumulative effect of even a 3 hour time change may affect healing rates due to the stress of internal and external desynchronization. Other stresses of travel include nutrition, hydration and destination (new site) stress as well as physiological separation from friends and family.

Your body's clock is managed by a small sector of the brain that controls the timing of biological functions like sleeping and eating and sets the peak times for your mind and body. The body's

Fig. 11.26

*Sprint on golf course*

Fig. 11.27

*Pool sprints*

clock is designed for a regular cycle of daylight and darkness. This biological cycle becomes out of sync by changing time zones and is completely confused when it experiences daylight and darkness at the "wrong" times in a new time zone.

The more time zones you cross, the greater the disruption to your body's clock. It may take the body's clock a week to adjust to travel across five time zones (Eastern South America or the USA to Western Europe). Minimizing the effects of jet lag and immediately adjusting to the current time zone will help resynchronize the athlete.

**Practical Application** (Fit to Play-Jet Lag Protocol) Try a dynamic warm-up of about 10–15 minutes. Follow this with a light 15–20 minute run or 20–25 minute cycle. Do 5 x 20 meter running sprints or 5 x 30 second cycle sprints or pool run sprints *(See Fig. 11.26 / 11.27)* about 4 hours before bed. This releases muscle protein in the blood and helps trigger the sleep mechanism. If a sauna or

whirlpool is available, use it (see Reinvigorate with Recovery menu for ideas). Be sure to drink plenty of fluids to make up for those lost in the sauna.

# Conclusion

Many practical solutions can be implemented by the athletes and with the help of a physical therapist. Proper recovery depends on many factors and individuals who know and understand this can selectively apply techniques on an individual basis to facilitate recovery and improve performance.

The challenge for most athletes, coaches and therapists and is to identify which specific capacities are fatigued and then select appropriate recovery strategies to restore the athlete to a normal functioning state. We all need to be more aware of the importance of implementing the 'rules of recovery' following heavy workloads and how best to use the equipment, facilities and modalities available to us. It is important to educate athletes, coaches, parents and others who work with athletes about the need to integrate recovery time and appropriate strategies into training on a regular basis.

Without the implementation of appropriate short term recovery strategies including adequate rest, athletes may not adapt to the stresses of training, practice, competition, travel, lifestyle, environment and other health stressors and may experience overtraining or overuse injuries. By following the short and long term recovery strategies outlined in this chapter on a consistent daily, weekly and monthly basis athletes can train hard stay Fit to Play™ Golf and ensure healthy high performance training and competition.

# Publishing Information

## PUBLISHING INFORMATION

Fit to Play™ Golf
Stuttgart: Neuer Sportverlag, 2018

**Authors**
Carl Petersen
#1303-289 Drake St., Vancouver, BC.
Canada V6B 5Z5
Nina Nittinger
Horlaubenstr. 2c, 7260 Davos, Switzerland

**Project Management and Editor**
Hendrik Schulze Kalthoff, Nadine Müller

**Design**
Pars pro toto Advertising Agency, Nadine Müller
www.parsprototo.com

**Publisher**
Neuer Sportverlag
Silberburgstr. 112, 70176 Stuttgart, Germany
Phone: +49 (0)711/66614-31
www.neuersportverlag.de

## PRODUCTION

**Layout and Typesetting**
Nadine Müller, Jens Ratzel, Kim Vollmer

**Reproduction and Picture Retouching**
Schwabenrepro GmbH
www.schwabenrepro.de

**Print**
Medienrad Production
www.medienrad.de

## PHOTO CREDITS

Hendrik Schulze Kalthoff
Nina Nittinger
Carl Petersen
Nick Saager

## MODEL CREDITS

Nina Nittinger
Nadine Müller
Nick Saager
Carl Petersen

## SELECTED REFERENCES

Akuthota V, Nadler SE. (2004) Core strengthening. Arch Phys Med Rehabil; 85 (3 Suppl 1); S86-92.

Alyas, F et al. (2007) MRI finding in lumbar spine of asymptomatic, adolescent elite tennis players. Br J Sports med;41:836-841.

Bar-Or O. (2001) Nutritional considerations for the child athlete. Can J Appl Physiol. 26:186-191.

Bompa T. (1985) Theory and methodology of training – the key to athletic performance. Dubuque: Kendall/Hunt, 1985.

Borg, G. A.V. (1982) Psychophysical bases of perceived exertion. Med. Sci. Sports Exerc. 14(5), 377-381.

Brukner P, Khan K. (2002) Principles of injury prevention in clinical sports medicine. Roseville: McGraw Hill Australia Pty Ltd.

Celebrini, R. (2001). Illustration from lecture on The Athlete Self Screening Exam™. Vancouver, Canada (Spring)

Costill DL, Hargreaves M. (1992) Carbohydrate nutrition and fatigue. Sports Med.;13(2):86-92.

Coyle EF.(1995) Substrate utilization during exercise in active people. Am J Clin Nutr. 61:S968-S979

De Mey K, Danneels L, Cagnie B, Lotte VD, Johan F, Cools AM. (2012) Kinetic chain influences on upper and lower trapezius muscle activation during eight variations of a scapular retraction exercise in overhead athletes. J Sci Med Sport. May 31

Enoka, R.M. (1994). Neuromechanical Basis of Kinesiology. Champaign, IL: Human Kinetics.

Goldbeck, TG, Davies GJ. (2000) Test-retest reliability of the closed kinetic chain upper extremity stability test. Journal of Sports Rehabilitation.

Granter, R. (2002). Principles of treatment. In: Brukner & Khan (Eds). Clinical Sports Medicine (Revised 2nd edition) 151. Roseville: McGraw Hill Australia Pty Ltd.

Hartig, D.E., Henderson, J.M. (1999) Increasing hamstring flexibility decreases lower extremity injuries in military basic trainees. Am. J. Sports Med. 27(2): 173-176.

Ireland ML, Willson JD, Ballantyne BT, McClay Davis I. (2003) Hip Strength in Females With and Without Patellofemoral Pain. J Ortho Sports Phys Ther. Vol. 33, No. 11. November.

Juett,T. (1988). Myofascial release: an introduction for the patient. Phys.Ther. 7(41): 78.

Kellman, M. (2003) Underrecovery and Overtraining – Different Concepts Similar Impact. Olympic Coach Summer, Vol.18, No.3 page-4-7 U.S. Olympic Committee, Colorado Springs, Colorado.

Lee, D. (1999). Postpartum Health for Moms. www.dianelee.ca/postpartum/

Lucas, R.C. & Koslow R. (1984) Comparative study of static, dynamic and proprioceptive neuromuscular facilitation stretching techniques on flexibility. Percept Mot Skills. 58:615-618.

Petersen, C. & Sirdevan, M. (2006) Chapter 26-Core Training to Hold Neutral in Petersen, C & Nittinger, N. Fit to Play-Tennis: High Performance Training Tips. Racquet Tech Publishing, Vista, California, USA.

Leetun DT, Ireland ML, Wislon JD et al. (2004) Core stability measures as risk factor for lower extremity injury in athletes. Med Sci Sports Exerc 36 (6); 926-34

Maenhout A, Van Praet K, Pizzi L, VanHerzeele M, Cools A. (2009) Electromyographic analysis of knee push up plus variations: what's the influence of the kinetic chain on scapular muscle activity? Br J Sports med, Published Online First: 14 September 2009 doi:10.1136/bjsm.2009.062810

Petersen C. (2005) Fit to play: practical tips for faster recovery (part 1). J Medicine & Science in Tennis; (10) 1.

Petersen C. (2006a) Fit to Play-Recovery Tips (part 2) Medicine & Science in Tennis; Vol.10, No. 2.

Petersen, C. (2006b) Chapter 5 Balance Training in C. Petersen & N. Nittinger-Fit to Play-Tennis' High Performance Training Tips' Racquet Tech Publishing, Vista, California, USA.

Petersen, C. & Nittinger, N. (2006) Fit to Play-Tennis: High Performance Training Tips. Racquet Tech Publishing, Vista, California, USA.

Prentice, W.E. (1983). A comparison of static and PNF stretching for improving hip joint flexibility. Athletic Training. 18(1): 56-59.

Racquet Tech Publishers diagrams 1st published in C. Petersen & N, Nittinger Fit to Play -Tennis 2006. Birmingham, Alabama.

Richardson CA, Jull GA, Hodges PW, Hides J. (1999). Therapeutic Exercise for Spinal Segmental Stabilization in Low Back Pain. Churchill-Livingstone.

Schamberger W. (2002) The malalignment syndrome-implications for medicine and sport. London: Churchill Livingstone.

Snijders C J, Vleeming A, Stoeckart R (1993) Transfer of lumbo-sacral load to iliac bones and legs. 1: Biomechanics of self-bracing of the sacroiliac joints and its significance for treatment and exercise. Clinical Biomechanics 8:285

Soleway, C. (2001). Body Therapy–Small Ball Release Program. Longmont, Colorado: Ball Dynamics International. (website: www.fitball.com)

Steindler, A. (1955) Kinesiology of the Human Body. Springfield, Ill: Charles C. Thomas.

Travell, J.G., Simons, D.G. (1998). Myofascial Pain and Dysfunction–The Trigger Point Manual, Vol. 2. (2nd edition). Maryland:Williams & Wilkins.

Vleeming A, Pool-Goudzwaard A L, Stoeckart R, Wingerden J P van, Snijders C J (1995) The posterior layer of the thoracolumbar fascia: its function in load transfer from spine to legs. Spine 20 : 753-758

Wenger, H.A. (1986). Personal communication.

Witkorsson-Moller, M., Oberg, B., Ekstrand, J., Gillquist, J. (1983). Effects of warming up, massage and stretching on range of motion and muscle strength in the lower extremity. Am. J. Sports Med. 11(4): 249-52.

# NEUER SPORTVERLAG

# Mental Training for Your Best Golf Game

To each player, anyone from the club player with a green card and the junior national team players to the professional players, 18 holes on the golf course equal 18 challenges. This does not only refer to technical and tactical skills, but especially for the mind, golf psychology starts long before the first hole.

The mentally oriented golf training presented in this practical exercise book covers the buildup of the mental skills in order to be able to keep these balanced when put under pressure at competitions and stressful situations. Thanks to this book each player should be able to top his or her performance when it matters.

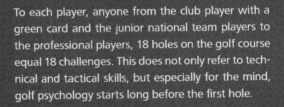

**Mental Training for Your Best
Golf Game**

17 x 24 cm, colored, 192 pages, paperback
ISBN 978-3-944526-27-0
ISBN 978-3-944526-59-1

### Nina Nittinger

Certified A license coach in physical conditioning and tennis. Former Fitness Coach Swiss Golf Association. Being on tour for years as a tennis pro, she studied sports management and sports psychology after her tennis career.

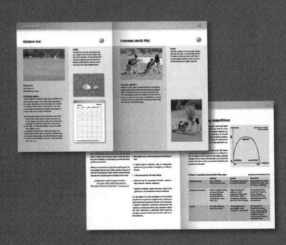

| | | | |
|---|---|---|---|
| **Book** | 19,50 € | 19,50 € | amazon.com |
| **eBook** | 9,99 €<br>12,99 $* | | Download on iBooks / amazonkindle |

*\* Prices may vary due to local taxes.*

Neuer Sportverlag | Silberburgstr. 112 | 70176 Stuttgart | Germany | info@neuersportverlag.de | www.neuersportverlag.de

NEUER SPORTVERLAG

# by Nina Nittinger

## Said about the book

"To play golf is a long road on which you invest a lot of energy in order to find answers and solutions for the most diverse tasks. This book can assist any player with valuable and still simple tools in order to develop his or her game as successfully and mentally strong as possible."

Paolo Quirici, previous golf professional, sports director ASG (Swiss Golf Association)

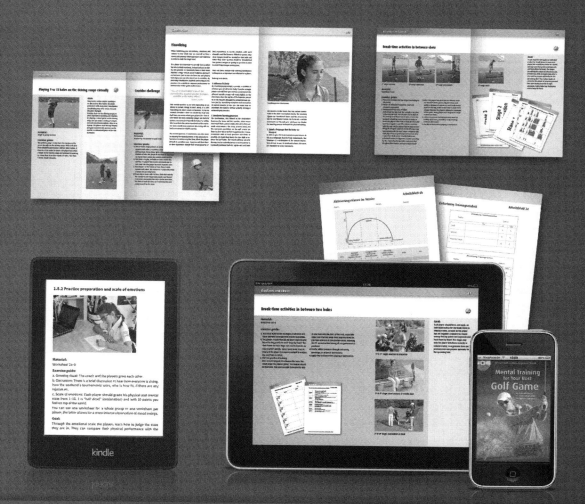

Neuer Sportverlag | Silberburgstr. 112 | 70176 Stuttgart | Germany | info@neuersportverlag.de | www.neuersportverlag.de

# NEUER SPORTVERLAG

## www.my-pocket-coach.com

**My-Pocket-Coach Fitness** is a dynamic fitness training series that includes multi-core exercises for both upper and lower body. It is a useful training tool for athletes and individuals of all ages and varied fitness levels from developing athletes to adults. If you are looking for innovative, evidence based exercises to enhance your training routine this is the perfect fitness coach for you. It targets functional exercises that work the bodies muscle slings in closed and partially closed kinetic chain movements.

This series initially focuses on **'Basework & Bridging'** exercises in lying, supine, prone, quadruped and seated bridge positions to form the foundation of your core stability training. The exercises then progress to **'Balls & Bands'** offering the user a practical, hands-on approach using elastic resistance, medicine balls, physio balls and balance equipment to provide enhanced functional core stability training. The next progressions further improve three dimensional core stability by **'Connecting the Core'** with a variety of sport specific exercises in different squat positions. The final exercises focus on upper core and shoulder stability to help enhance rotator cuff stability.

The complete **My-Pocket-Coach Series** is available as eBook on Apple iBooks. In addition, My-Pocket-Coach Fitness is available as a printed training cards set at **www.my-pocket-coach.com**. My-Pocket-Coach Tennis and Psyched up are available as paperback at **www.amazon.com**.

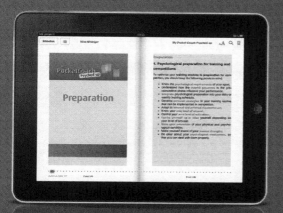

### The Authors

**Nina Nittinger**
Certified A license coach in physical conditioning and tennis.

**Carl Petersen**
Physiotherapist / Director of High Performance Training

Neuer Sportverlag | Silberburgstr. 112 | 70176 Stuttgart | Germany | info@neuersportverlag.de | www.neuersportverlag.de

NEUER SPORTVERLAG

# Fit To Play™ & Perform

closed and partially closed kinetic chain movements. Functional core stability training with a physio ball, balance equipment, medicine ball and stretch bands strengthens the lower core and legs in all planes of motion.

### Set 2 –Core Stability 1 – Basework & Bridging & Core Stability 4 – Connecting Your Core
Core Stability 1 takes you through a series of innovative exercises to enhance your training routine and challenge your core stability in three dimensions and multiple planes of movement. This DVD focuses on exercises in lying, supine, prone, quadruped and seated bridge positions to form the foundation of your core stability training. The exercises are practical, versatile and can be done anywhere with minimal equipment.

**Fit to Play™ & Perform 2 DVD sets.**
**Set 1 -Agility Drills & Core Stability 2 –**
**Lower Core & Legs**
Agility Drills gets you the performance benefits of sports specific agility, balance & coordination drills. This innovative DVD includes a high performance warm-up and offers dozens of drills to challenge footwork, improve multi-directional quickness, reaction time and explosive power to enhance athletic performance. This comprehensive DVD offers the user a practical, hands-on approach using ladders, cones, balance equipment, elastic resistance, medicine balls, hurdles and much more to provide fast feet training applicable to athletes of all ages.

Core Stability 2 improves your three dimensional core stability by connecting the lower core and legs with functional exercises that work the muscle slings in

Core Stability 4 improves your three dimensional core stability by connecting the upper and lower core with functional exercises that utilize common gym equipment in closed and partially closed kinetic chain movements. Functional core stability training with a pullies, physio ball, balance equipment, and stretch bands improves stability of the upper and lower core connection.

The functional core stability exercises shown in these 2 set DVD series help ensure optimal recruitment, balance, timing, deceleration control, performance, and injury prevention. These exercises are versatile, practical, transportable, and affordable. These DVD's are appropriate for multiple activities and sports and can be used by active people and athletes of all ages.

Fit to Play DVD sets are available here: **www.ninisports.com** (Shipping Europe) **fit2playcarl@gmail.com** (Shipping Canada/US)

# About the Authors

Carl Petersen
BPE, BSc(PT)

Nina Nittinger
Dipl. KFFR Sports Management

## CARL PETERSEN

Carl is a partner and international travel consultant at City Sports & Physiotherapy clinic in Vancouver, Canada. He has treated and trained athletes and weekend warriors worldwide from a variety of sports keeping them Fit to Play™ & Perform for over 30 years. Carl is an internationally recognized and sought after speaker. He is regularly found educating physicians, physiotherapists, coaches, and athletes around the world on the principles of keeping Fit to Play™. He has written over 300 professional articles and has written and co-authored a number of books, DVD's and other training resources. In 2007, he was the recipient of the Physiotherapy Association of BC "Award of Excellence for Clinical Contribution". Carl is looking forward to spending increased time on the golf course in the near future.

**www.citysportsphysio.com**
On twitter @Fit2PlayCarl
email: fit2playcarl@gmail.com

## NINA NITTINGER

Nina Nittinger studied sports and business management after finishing her career as a professional tennis player. Alongside her studies she also completed studies in sports psychology. She is a certified A license coach in physical conditioning and tennis.

As an author of many books, three My-Pocket-Coach training card sets and more than 40 professional articles on fitness and mental training she has made a name for herself and has been invited to talk at various national and international conferences.

Alongside her company ninisports she worked as a regional coach fitness for the Swiss Golf Association (ASG) since 2012. She is a passionate player with a current handicap of 5.8.

**www.ninisports.com**